REMNANTS

and

What Remains

Made in Michigan Writers Series

A complete listing of the books in this series can be found online at wsupress.wayne.edu.

Praise for *REMNANTS and What Remains*

"A profoundly moving, insightful, and—above all—humane work. Greenspan does not simply tell but shows us what it means to engage with survivors, as he has done in sustained and deepening conversations over decades."

—Dan Stone, professor of modern history, University of London

"One comes away from reading this work with the sense of having just sat at the feet of a distinguished elder, as he makes his thinking visible in this profoundly personal volume. We are so often delighted by his keen wit or made *faklempt* by the depth of his response. I daresay that Dr. Hank Greenspan's penetrating reflections in and on practice will encourage all of us to have the courage to cultivate such critical professional and personal connections in our own lives."

—Belarie Zatzman, professor of theater, York University

"This moving autobiographical narrative about Hank Greenspan's 'moments from a life among Holocaust survivors' stands with the legendary testimony of Primo Levi and Jean Améry. What remains from Greenspan's exceptional playwriting and performance, from his lifelong listening and deep recounting includes this classic—a book bound for intense reading and ongoing study as it connects memory and memorial, making loss and resistance against it inseparable."

—John K. Roth, author of *Sources of Holocaust Insight*

"In *REMNANTS and What Remains*, Henry Hank Greenspan weaves his decades of deepening conversations with Holocaust survivors into a deeply personal reflection on the ethical and emotional challenges of listening, remembering, and retelling. As an oral historian, playwright, actor, and psychologist, Greenspan continues to bring innovative approaches to the ways we engage with memory."

—Jeffrey Veidlinger, director, Raoul Wallenberg Institute, University of Michigan

"Hank has championed the art of hearing 'with' Holocaust survivors rather than solely from them, his approach resting on the relationships he has built over decades. Hank not only tells us his sensitively observed interpretations but, as a playwright, he shows us. This book is evidence of Hank's deeply profound impact on the field of Holocaust studies and on humanity itself."

—Christine Schmidt, The Wiener Holocaust Library, London

"This is a gift. What Hank offers are not simple testimonies but rather stories that emerge over time. They constitute over fifty years of intimate conversations about love and loss, friendship, and life before and after the Holocaust. The book is at once an intimate memorial and a tribute to those who lived on."

—Laura Levitt, author of *The Objects That Remain* and *American Jewish Loss After the Holocaust*

"A profoundly human and accessible work. Reading *REMNANTS* made me want to perform it, in a way that I rarely want to perform a text."

—Lisa Peschel, professor of theater, University of York

"Anyone who has been fortunate enough to be in the audience of a performance of *REMNANTS* has encountered the unexpected gift of Greenspan sharing his lifetime of conversations with Holocaust survivors as theater. This publication guarantees that the play will reach an audience of readers for years to come. And *What Remains* extends the play's deep engagement with survivors' stories by inspiring all of us to embrace listening and sitting with complexity."

—Alexandra Garbarini, Hans W. Gatzke '38 Professor of Modern European History and Jewish studies at Williams College

REMNANTS and What Remains

Moments from a Life Among Holocaust Survivors

Henry Hank Greenspan

WAYNE STATE UNIVERSITY PRESS
DETROIT

ISBN 9780814352632 (paperback)
ISBN 9780814352649 (ebook)

Library of Congress Control Number: 2025931228

Cover illustration and design by Lindsey Cleworth.

Publication of this book was made possible by a generous gift from The Meijer Foundation.

Wayne State University Press rests on Waawiyaataanong, also referred to as Detroit, the ancestral and contemporary homeland of the Three Fires Confederacy. These sovereign lands were granted by the Ojibwe, Odawa, Potawatomi, and Wyandot Nations, in 1807, through the Treaty of Detroit. Wayne State University Press affirms Indigenous sovereignty and honors all tribes with a connection to Detroit. With our Native neighbors, the press works to advance educational equity and promote a better future for the earth and all people.

Wayne State University Press
Leonard N. Simons Building
4809 Woodward Avenue
Detroit, Michigan 48201-1309

Visit us online at wsupress.wayne.edu.

To the memory of Sid Bolkosky, my best friend, comrade in Lagavulin, and brother in every other sense of spirit

Contents

Introduction

VOICES

Scholarly books often begin with an amusing anecdote. It helps prepare readers for the thicker stuff to follow.

This book moves in the opposite direction. It is a work of literature—both a playscript and excerpts from a memoir that is a spoken-word piece as well as a text. Above all, this is a book of voices: others' and my own.

REMNANTS, the play, is based on what is now fifty years of listening to Holocaust survivors—not in single interviews, but in deepening conversations with the same survivors sustained over months, years, sometimes decades. The first iteration of the play was produced for radio in 1991 and distributed on National Public Radio (NPR) in the United States. For radio, *REMNANTS* was subtitled "a voice play." Even now, more than three hundred onstage performances later, I would say it is still a voice play. It is as much about *how* survivors retell as what; the ways survivors construct an account as much as the account itself.

Most essentially, *REMNANTS* recreates moments in which survivors struck on an image or anecdote—often to their own surprise—that seemed to nail what they wished to convey, both about their lives during the war and after. The dramatic action is survivors finding and developing such images and the relationship that each survivor works to establish with their listeners.

That relationship is different for each survivor represented, as is the emotional tone and narrative style of each segment of the piece.

The survivors in *REMNANTS* are thus particular people speaking in particular circumstances. They are not iconic "witnesses" providing fragments of iconic "testimony." My favorite response to the play is when an audience member says, "It was not what I expected." I have learned that our expectations of what survivors have to retell, and about survivors themselves, is a fence that is not easy to get around. And so I am particularly pleased when *REMNANTS* manages to move audiences beyond it.

What Remains is retold in my own voice as I look back on experiences with survivors—in most cases, on full relationships—which underlie both *REMNANTS* and my life's work as a whole. My conversations with survivors—and my teaching and writing about those conversations—began long before I imagined a play. Being a scholar/teacher and a playwright/actor came to evolve together. Here, I clarify some of the connections.

Approaching the end of my career as both scholar and playwright, *What Remains* has been a chance to remember, celebrate, and grieve. These days, there has been a near obsession with keeping survivors alive, not only in voice but in three-dimensional presence—through interactive video technology, through the accounts of survivors' children and grandchildren, and even through work like *REMNANTS*. We imagine enlisting survivors, or their surrogates, in the struggle against antisemitism and hatred in general. But the reality, as *What Remains* conveys, is that, at the end of their lives, most survivors look to the past and not the future, to the worlds to which they once belonged and that are now mostly erased.

They look for traces of the home they knew before they became its remnants.

Much as we can learn from survivors—and there is an enormous amount to learn from survivors—their experiences and reflections are not enough to tell us how to navigate the multiple catastrophes of our own time. Survivors can be our teachers, but I don't think they can be our guides. As Agi Rubin put it, a survivor whose voice you will come to know well, "In the end, my legacy is not up to me. It is up to whoever comes after, to pick up this bit, remember that part . . . as it may apply to their own circumstances, which I know will be different from mine."

ORIGINS

When I began my conversations with survivors in the 1970s, I was not thinking about a play or performance of any kind. While playwrights often do research for a piece, I was doing research only to do research, as I still do today.

It was only after two decades of interviewing survivors, reading Holocaust history and memoirs, and teaching the Holocaust that I found myself ready, almost against my inclination, to try a dramatic piece. The idea was suggested by a student theater group who knew about my work and asked if I could write a Holocaust-related play for them. I initially said, "No." I genuinely did not think I was capable. But there were certain things I had learned and heard that made me want to show as well as tell. And, it turns out, my way of engaging survivors, what I call my practice, was well suited for such an effort. The first version of *REMNANTS* was the result.

I have often said that I was lucky to begin my conversations with survivors in the 1970s. At that time, there were few models of what an interview with a survivor was supposed to look like.

While there was a range of earlier projects in which survivors' accounts were gathered, the approach that became near universal in the 1980s and '90s—a two-to-three-hour single interview, usually with a stranger, now usually videotaped—did not yet exist. That meant that survivors and I were free to make it up as we went along; in essence, to wing it. Part of what we "winged" was to meet as often and for as long as seemed useful—from a few weeks to a few decades. My training as a psychologist certainly influenced my inclination toward sustained conversation, but none of my work with survivors was part of any psychotherapy. Rather, multiple meetings were initially suggested by survivors themselves. Many said some version of "come back next week; we'll talk again; we'll talk some more." And so we did, creating a practice together.

Sustained conversations allowed me to listen to my audio recordings between meetings. This "listening to the listening" is critically important. One often hears things missed in the original interview while immersed in the conversational flow. I have often said that the much romanticized notion of deep listening is best realized in the unglamourous work of *re*listening—and taking the time to do it well.

I also did my own transcribing, which requires listening over and over to the same segment of an interview. This practice turned out to be essential in all my attempts to hear survivors well. But one immediate result was that, with repeated listening, survivors' voices—their various uses of silence, intonation, emphasis, rhythm, cadence, phrasing, and more—became essentially imprinted for me. So when I came to craft a voice play, I had an orchestra of distinct voices on which to draw.

Transcribing, of course, is humbling. One hears all one didn't hear or didn't hear well. Interviews always include roads not taken or even imagined, as well as obvious wrong turns and missed directions. Therefore, it mattered to know that there would be a next meeting in which to refine understanding.

As my practice developed, I came to bring recorded segments of earlier interviews to later ones—easy to do with audio recording—so that the survivors and I could revisit them together. Poring over these excerpts in tandem was an extraordinary experience. Besides clarification, the process typically sparked new memories and insights nowhere evident, and probably nonexistent, in earlier conversations. As Agi described:

> One thought sparks another, and then another, that I may not have even known I had. That is the part that is so gratifying. Whatever I think I'm teaching, I'm learning at the same moment. We're learning together.

"Learning together" grounded collaboration between survivors and myself. In different ways and to different degrees, survivors and I became partners and confidants. And that made all the difference in what they shared as well as in the depth and breadth of our conversations.

Like most interviews with survivors, mine usually began with survivors retelling a rough chronology of wartime experiences—where they were, some of what happened, how liberation came. Unlike most testimony projects, however, these accounts were only the *beginning* of our conversations. From there, many questions followed: Can it be retold? Can others understand? How does one choose what to retell and not tell—when, where, with whom? What has been the range of listeners' responses? Did you want to talk about it? Did others want to hear? What does it mean to be a "Holocaust survivor"—to oneself and, as perceived, to others? What has been the personal impact of living through and after the destruction—for oneself, one's family, and—as observed—for other survivors? What has been the impact of the Holocaust on the world? Has it mattered? How so (and how not so)? What about faith—in divinity? In humanity? What about having, or not having, children? What about getting up in the morning? What about death? What about anticipating one's own death? What about the world's future? What about what remains, or does not remain, of the world that was?

As these questions suggest, my conversations with survivors have been as much oral psychology, oral philosophy, oral political reflection, and oral narratology (all the questions about retelling) as oral history. Those were the issues I wanted to raise, and, in most cases, they were what survivors wanted to discuss, especially as we got to know each other well. And, of course, in our deepening conversations, the format was not simply question followed by answer. Rather, it was reflection and revision over time. In contrast with conventional testimonies and single interviews more generally, exploration far outweighed declaration.

Much in our conversations was about survivors' experiences with listeners, and listeners are central in both my scholarly and dramatic writing. It is mostly not good news. While contemporary scholarship has suggested that the early isolation of survivors—stigmatized, avoided, or directly silenced—is a kind of myth, none of the survivors I've known would agree. A surprising number spontaneously recalled the saying, "When you laugh, the whole world laughs with you. And when you cry, you cry alone." Agi, Abe, Reuben, and others you will meet followed with some version of, "And that's exactly what we did."

Indeed, there was a lot in our early conversations that was at least gently subversive, not only about whether there were interested listeners but about what "we"—the big cultural "we"—presumed about survivors. I have noted my particular pleasure when I hear audiences tell me that *REMNANTS* is "not what I expected," and survivors who know the piece share my satisfaction in popping a few presumptive balloons. Still, almost none of the survivors I've known carry bitterness. They get that what they experienced, and what they know, is hard to get. And some of my fondest memories are survivors like Agi working on my own cynical tendencies. "You have to find the good, do what you can in the given circumstances. Improvise. That's what helped us survive." She also acknowledged that improvising wasn't always possible, but, on the other hand, she survived. "I'm as corny as Kansas in August!" she once exclaimed, inviting me to spend more of my own emotional time in the sunlight. It is a forever cherished memory that an Auschwitz survivor instructed me with a lyric from *South Pacific*.

Unexpected juxtapositions play a central role in my work, and especially in *REMNANTS*. Bali Hai does not appear, but there are space aliens, Native American dolls, Norman Cousins, how-to-survive guides for every life contingency, and a vanity in a latrine. These are some of the analogies, images, and fragments that survivors drew upon—usually in the moment—within our conversations. While they came from survivors, none of them are iconic Holocaust images—barbed wire, chimneys, barking dogs, or guards. Their centrality in *REMNANTS* is another way the play violates our usual expectations.

While aware of that, I was not looking for the exotic. When I introduce the play, I remind people of their own most memorable conversations with close friends. Every now and then, a friend will tell a story—often one they've shared with us many times before—but suddenly their retelling drops us through the floor. These are rare moments. Whether our friend unearths a striking image, a new insight, or simply a different-than-usual cadence of voice, such accounts seem to get to the heart. When I worked as a psychotherapist, clients often teared in the wake of such a story or realization, not usually because it was sad but because it was *true*—at least as true as what they could express at that moment. Their tears, I think, signified relief: relief that they finally found a way to really say it, and that someone else was there to hear.

For the listener, such moments are gifts. They usually depend on long acquaintance but are unanticipated—really, impossible to anticipate—even in that context. I have often described *REMNANTS* as a trajectory of such gifts. I would describe *What Remains* as stories about my relationships with those who bestowed them.

The gifts and the stories are themselves part of what remains.

REMNANTS

Overview

TITLE

Since *REMNANTS* was first produced for radio in 1991, and through more than three hundred stage performances since, its title has been in all caps. While there are exceptions, plays—like books—are usually in title case, and so *REMNANTS* would be *Remnants*. The all-caps spelling was a deliberate choice. Indeed, it is a microcosm of the whole play.

Remnants, like *Survivors*, suggests a group, a category of people. That is typically how we view survivors, at least those we don't know personally: not as individuals but as a collective representing the destruction they endured. Agi once exclaimed: "I am *not* a quote-unquote, capital *S*, 'Holocaust Survivor.' OK, I survived. But I am not *The* Survivor. I am not a category. Not a thing. We have enough experience being categories."

If only symbolically, the all-caps spelling of *REMNANTS* is intended to suggest the individuality of each survivor represented. They are not simply a collection, as *Survivors* might suggest, but particular people, each with their own style, tone, and way of engaging their listeners. While the play does have a trajectory that links the individual accounts we hear, that does not dilute the claim—and, I've learned, the impact—of each voice along the way.

REMNANTS is thus more mosaic than linear unfolding. Structurally, each piece "deserves" its own capital letter just as each segment has its own title. In a phrase I use in a different book, *REMNANTS* is a "gathering" of voices. It is not a chorus.

Meanwhile, there is another reason that the play is called *REMNANTS*—however spelled—rather than *Survivors*. Historically, the word goes back to what survivors called themselves in many of the Displaced Persons camps after liberation—*she'eret haplaytah* in Hebrew—the "surviving remnant." In truth, when I was writing the play, I was not thinking of that reference; the title floated up from wherever titles come. But I did know that "survivors" would be a wrong choice. Horrific as their experiences may be—an assault, a plane crash, a natural disaster—survivors of such catastrophes are rarely also remnants of a destroyed world, a "*whole* way of life" as described by one survivor whom you will hear. At least in this way, survivors of genocide are different from survivors of other hells. Again, Agi: "The life I was made to live is gone. I am alive. In another life." And so also the first line of *REMNANTS*: "The voices of Holocaust survivors are themselves survivors. Each must draw on words and cadences that once belonged to entire communities, even while retelling how those communities were destroyed."

STRUCTURE AND SYNOPSIS

REMNANTS is a stark, minimalist trajectory of seven monologues (four women, three men) now usually presented as a one-person performance by the author. The play reflects fifty years of deepening conversations between the playwright and a small group of Holocaust survivors. *REMNANTS* is not survivor testimony. Rather, it recreates specific moments when survivors struck on an image or anecdote that nailed their experience as much about their lives since the war as during. Moments of such clarity and candor are rare in any conversation. They are gifts.

The dramatic action of the piece is the process of retelling itself: survivors' landing on such images, their deployment and development, and the relationship that each survivor works to establish with the audience. The quality of that relationship is different in each monologue, as is the emotional tone, narrative voice, and personal style. What is consistent is that each segment, and the piece as a whole, challenges much of what we think we know about the Holocaust and about its survivors. Survivors' efforts to retell are burdened not only by horrific memories and losses. They are also burdened by listeners who assume there is nothing new to learn. *REMNANTS* eschews, and sometimes directly contests, such presumptions.

Along with survivors' efforts to retell, there is, implicitly, the playwright's. When I perform the piece, I do not view myself as "playing" survivors. Rather, I am doing what we all do when we relay what one friend has told us to a second friend. When we convey "what Jane said," we usually "do Jane" to some extent—incorporating some of her gestures, patterns of speech, and narrative style. Rather than relaying a verbatim transcript, we paraphrase the gist of what Jane said. One survivor represented in *REMNANTS*, when asked by a reporter whether the play includes "exactly what you said to Hank," responded: "It's not exactly what I said, but it's exactly what I meant." I'll take that as good enough.

A performance of *REMNANTS* lasts about forty-five minutes—potentially an awkward length. But it is almost always followed by discussion—what I call "talk with" rather than "talk back"—which typically lasts just as long. These post-performance conversations allow me to draw on what I've learned over all these years of listening to, teaching about, and writing about the Holocaust and survivors.

HISTORY

REMNANTS was not written for radio but, by chance, was first produced in that medium at WUOM-FM at the University of Michigan. That program was picked up by NPR and APM stations around the country and broadcast roughly two hundred times in 1991 and 1992. It received two Michigan Public Radio Focus Awards, won the 1994 National Script Competition of the Midwest Radio Theatre Workshop, and was recognized nationally in two 1994 Commendation Awards from American Women in Radio and Television.

The radio cast—six actors doing what was then six monologues—was staged several times, and the script was also picked up by theaters and festivals around the country. The first Equity production was a two-week run at the New Hope Performing Arts Festival in 1995.

The first one-person production was a three-week run at the John Houseman Theater in New York in 1997. Since then, I have performed *REMNANTS* at more than three hundred venues worldwide.

Along with the recognition that the radio production received, *REMNANTS* was a winner of the New Hope Performing Arts Festival; the CenterPieces Reading Series of the Mill Mountain Theatre of Roanoke; the Henrico Theatre Company National Competition in Richmond, Virginia; the Attic Theatre Center of Los Angeles New Plays Festival; and the Pendragon Theater Festival of the Lakes in Saranac Lake, New York. This volume marks the first time the script has been published. A recent live performance streamed on Zoom from the 2022 Marsh International Solo Festival in San Francisco can be accessed at https://youtu.be/LVu8XhcMXjw. An in-studio performance video can be accessed at https://youtu.be/Vty8b_euk-k.

PRODUCTION NOTES

These notes apply most directly to the one-person performance, although, as noted, *REMNANTS* has been performed by an ensemble of actors.

The piece has been presented in theaters, auditoria, church and synagogue sanctuaries, museums, and, most memorably, in the Magdeburg Attic Theatre of the former Theresienstadt ghetto, a space used for rehearsal and performance during the Holocaust itself. (That performance is remembered in *What Remains*.) In keeping with its minimalist style, *REMNANTS* has minimal requirements. Essentially, it can be done in any space.

Adding music or "Holocaust-associated" objects or images (stars, barbed wire, train sounds, etc.) is almost always a bad idea. Likewise, any hackneyed heaviness: all-black clothing or similar. Less is always more—certainly, for this piece; I would say for Holocaust representations in general. One theater in Los Angeles dressed all the actors in striped prison uniforms (even though they were survivors and some had never been in a camp), put numbers on their arms (even though a small fraction of survivors—only those in Auschwitz—ever had tattooed numbers), and spoke in some version of an Elie Wiesel accent—all over-the-top.

Turning survivors into Holocaust figurines is the opposite of the spirit and goals of *REMNANTS*. They should wear what, for that person, fits the occasion and the implicit setting—in a school auditorium or similar public setting, in intimate conversation, etc. (See notes for each monologue.) Some of the monologues are inward. Others are the opposite. Most are a combination of both.

When I do the piece as a solo performance, I do not use blackouts between monologues, and there is no change of set or costume. Often, I have the script on a music stand to the side. I don't read from it, but I turn the pages between monologues to signal the transition (and provide some time, for both myself and the audience, to make the turn). I have learned that these transitions are a key part of the piece—who is going to appear next? Each monologue has its own title, which I say at its start, as well as the gender of the speaker. Gender is clear enough in the writing, but I have found that taking the question off the table enhances audience focus.

This also reminds an audience that they are watching me aiming to convey "what Jane said"—again, as opposed to "playing Jane." The undisguised presence of the "real guy"—who knows the person whose voice, feelings, and style he is sharing—grounds the piece as a whole.

With very few exceptions—such as purely memorial occasions—I always include a discussion after a *REMNANTS* performance. Not unusually, these can last as long as the play itself. They create a chance for the audience to respond immediately to the piece. And knowing some of the background of the play, to raise a wide range of questions: about my experiences writing and performing the piece, about survivors, and about contemporary issues an audience views as relevant.

TIME

Always the immediate present—that is, the performance itself—since the play is not situated during the war, nor within a particular conversation I had with a survivor, but in the moment I am sharing what I heard and learned from my survivor-friends with the audience. Of course, these other time contexts are layered into what is shared.

CHARACTER/VOICE NOTES FOR EACH MONOLOGUE

Voice (a woman, mid-forties): Subdued, self-contained, no frills. Rebuilt from muteness, her voice conveys only what is necessary. Best imagined in a small group setting, perhaps a few college students.

Mars (a man, mid-fifties): Engaging and curious. Soft rather than bitter irony at times; a person who takes no special pleasure in having to be ironic. Best imagined in a medium-sized hall, perhaps a synagogue.

Burying the Cemetery (a man, around sixty): Intellectual, precise. His goal is to define terms, establish facts. He knows that he alone is witness to the erasure of a community. His words are the cemetery. A very inward monologue, so wherever imagined he is mainly in his head.

Missing Persons (a woman, fifties): A confident narrator, clear-eyed, grounded. She could just as well be telling her own story. Perhaps she is. Best imagined in a large auditorium in which, at the end, she is lost.

Dolls (a woman, early fifties): An ingenue in ways that don't match all that is outrageous in her account. She carries a secret, which she eventually both reveals and retracts. Best imagined in a small gathering of friends.

How to Survive (a man, late fifties): A comedian who knows how to work his audience. He sets them up, almost literally, for the kill. The full-bore rage to which he eventually gives voice is both righteous and, as he shows physically, poison to carry. Best imagined with a large audience whom he works—until the rage works *him*.

The Vanity (a woman, late fifties): Both reticent and assertive, she finds her moments. She has learned to live without synthesis and resolution—without facile "lessons of the

Holocaust"—and wants to help us to do the same. Best to imagine anywhere truth is told.

Ages are what people roughly were when they first shared with me what they did, but, as above, the play takes place in the present moment in which I aim to convey some of what one group of my friends (the survivors) have to relay to another group of my friends (the audience).

TRAJECTORY

I am often asked why the monologues are in the order they are. There is a deliberate trajectory. In essence, each aims to challenge our usual stopping points in discussions of the Holocaust and its survivors. I have sometimes imagined *REMNANTS* as a series of closing doors. "No, you can't rest here. There is more to know; more to feel."

As examples, the first monologue—a woman's story of being literally muted during the war—ends with silence, a usual Holocaust trope. The monologue that immediately follows opens with a survivor saying, "In the beginning, we *wanted* to talk about it." So much for silence. He ends with an invocation of Mars. The camps being "another planet" is another part of conventional rhetoric. Thus, the next monologue graphically describes atrocity happening, not only *on* the earth, but *in* the earth. There is no other planet. That monologue ends with human ash, which is yet another usual stopping place. And so the monologue that follows evokes the memory of specific people—a "father who used to play a lot of soccer," a mother with "red hair and freckles." Not ash, but those who were once particular people. People exactly like ourselves. And so on.

While this trajectory is never explicitly stated in the play, my sense has been that audiences feel a closing in as the piece unfolds. It is intense and condensed, and that is deliberate. For some, it may be too unremitting—not because of horror; there is also humor in the play. But because—if I read the reviews and responses accurately—it is stark, spare, and honest.

Years ago, after writing the first version of *REMNANTS*, I thought of it as a kind of time capsule. I wanted it to be short and condensed because I didn't imagine that many people, beyond experts in this area, would have or take the time to immerse themselves seriously in the reality of the Holocaust and its survivors.

After all these years, I leave it to others to assess how much has changed.

REMNANTS

Narrator's Introduction

The voices of Holocaust survivors are themselves survivors.

Each must draw on words and cadences that once belonged to entire communities, even while retelling how those communities were destroyed.

And each must persist within a remembered terror that can still consume a voice, and sometimes does.

And each must anticipate that their truths will not be easily received.

REMNANTS is a gathering of such voices.

Voice
(a woman)

During the war, I lost my voice. I literally lost my voice. I was a little kid at the time. A little *pisher* like we say in Yiddish. I was eight years old. And at that time, I lost my voice.

This was in 1943. In the ghetto. It was after one of those *Aktions*—you know, when the SS come in and they kill a lot of people. And they round up the others, and they take them to the train. And the train takes them away.

After one of those *Aktions*, I lost my voice. I don't know why. But for two years, I did not speak a single word.

(*steps forward*)

After the war, my voice came back. Not right away, but very slowly. This was in 1945, in a DP camp, a camp for "displaced persons," mostly for Jews who had survived the war. During the day in that camp, I did not speak at all. But during the night, when I was having a nightmare, I screamed. So that was how we knew I still had a voice. Because during the day I was completely mute. But during the night, I screamed.

(*warming*)

There was a doctor at that camp, a Jewish doctor, who said: "If the girl can scream in the night, when she is asleep, so she can scream in the day, when she is awake. And if she can scream in the day, so she can also sing or cry. And if she can sing or cry, she can speak words as well. The voice can be salvaged. The screams can be refined into cries. And the cries can be refined into words."

So the doctor tried to help me. He took me to run in the hills near that camp. And he had me run with my mouth open so I could feel the air push up against my throat.

(*raises one hand to throat*)

And he told me to try to scream with the air in my throat. Or make any sound at all. And soon I *did* start to scream when I was running. And then I was crying and making other different sounds. And eventually the sounds became a voice. I could speak words again, after two years of no words at all.

(*Pause. Very still as at start.*)

Today, we have many words about the Holocaust. We argue, what does it mean? What should we do? What should we have done at the time? We argue for God and against Him. For Israel and against Israel. For reaching out to others and against reaching out to others. We argue and we reflect and we argue some more.

But to me, when I think about the Holocaust, I remember the doctor. And I remember myself, when I was a young girl, running in the hills.

Because to me, *all* our words, *whatever* we say about the Holocaust, are just so many different refinements of a cry. And the cry is just barely salvaged from a scream. And the scream is just barely salvaged from the silence.

Mars
(a man)

In the beginning, right after the war, we *wanted* to talk about it. I mean, if we could talk about it, we wanted to talk about it. We needed to talk about it. I wanted to talk about it a lot. But nobody wanted to hear.

Like, when I first came to this country, nobody wanted to hear about the Holo—, I mean, *nobody* wanted to hear about it. My own cousin, a dentist in California I met when I first came over here, he said to me—almost the first thing he said—he said, "Manny, I know what you went through. I saw the newsreels. I don't want to hear a word about it."

That's what he said to me. "I saw the newsreels."

(*steps forward*)

But, you know, a funny thing—to me, a funny thing I noticed that made me think: Maybe they *did* see something. This was 1947. Two years after the war. And I noticed—there were reports coming out, the first ones—about unidentified flying objects. Yeah! This was the beginning of all that with the Martians and the flying saucers. In 1947. Suddenly, in 1947, all these unidentified flying objects were showing up.

And then, just like they say today, some people were saying they saw the *people* from inside the spaceship. Yeah, just like they say today! They said they saw the people who were coming from Mars. And the people they saw had big, bald heads. And they had skinny arms and skinny legs. And large eyes, always the large eyes, in those big heads, on those skinny little bodies.

(*two beats*)

Now I said to myself: "I've seen these people before! Yeah! I've seen these people before! (*back there*) I've seen those thin, tiny, skinny bodies. I've seen those bald heads, bobbing up and down. I've seen those large eyes . . . eyes that were everywhere, staring, eyes seeing everything, seeing nothing . . ."

(*recovering*)

(*almost a bark*) Yeah! I've seen these people before. And my cousin, the dentist in California, he had also seen these people before. . . .

He saw them in the newsreels.

I saw them . . .

on Mars.

Burying the Cemetery

(a man)

(*a real question*) How do you destroy an entire people? Think about it. It's not an easy thing to do. It is not only killing millions of individuals, though it is certainly that. And it is not only degrading their culture, their way of life, though it is certainly also that. But to destroy a people, you have to wipe out every trace, the slightest possible trace, of their existence. You have to destroy *all* the evidence. Not only that they ever lived, but also that they ever died.

Late in the war, in one of the camps I was in, our job was to dig up the corpses of those whom the Germans had killed earlier. This happened in many of the places where they didn't have crematoria. There were mass graves, huge burial trenches, all over Poland and Russia and the Baltics. The people had been shot or gassed or just buried alive. They didn't want to waste bullets. Little children especially were often buried alive.

So our job was to dig up the corpses. And the German and Ukrainian guards screamed and beat us while we piled the bodies onto huge pyres. And then they poured gasoline on the bodies and set them on fire.

In this camp, even burning the bodies was not the end. They also took the gravestones from the Jewish cemeteries in that area. And many of the stones they had us break up, to turn them into gravel, to use to pave the muddy roads. And some were brought in to be stone platforms, like work benches, when we were burning the bodies.

After the bodies were burned, we had to collect all the ashes and put them on the work benches, on the gravestones. And if there were any large pieces of bone, or even little pieces, the SS made us grind them up. We had other pieces of stone from the gravestones, so we were able to grind all the pieces of bone into a fine gray powder.

The chief SS officer had a sieve that he carried, and all the prisoners had to bring him the ashes they had ground up. All the remains of the people had to be able to pass through the sieve.

At the end, the gravestones that we were using as work benches were also ground up. And the gravel and the ashes were mixed together with sand and spread around in the soil. Then more soil was added over that, and grass seed was laid down.

(*looking out over audience into distance*)

After a few weeks, the grass started coming up. It looked just like any other meadow. There was no sign that anything unusual had ever happened there.

And that's how the Germans murdered the murder of my people.

And how we buried the cemetery.

Missing Persons

(a woman)

Some of the stories we tell, some of the things that happened, even I myself find hard to believe.

Like, I have a very good friend—she was in Berlin, just outside Berlin, during the war. She was never sent to Auschwitz or any of the other camps. She was just living there, on false papers, with a false name and false identification.

She was not even from there. Her family were German-speaking Jews who lived in Czechoslovakia. So nobody in Berlin knew her. And they didn't know she was Jewish. To them, she was just a German girl working in a clothing factory, making uniforms, outside of Berlin.

In Czechoslovakia she had friends, non-Jewish friends, who were helping her parents. So she was able to find out what was going on. And she heard from these friends that her parents, and her little brother and sister, had been taken to Theresienstadt.

Theresienstadt was a camp, but it was not considered as bad. This was because the Germans kept it as a "show place"—(*with irony*) a camp where they "cared for" their prisoners.

But then, at the end of 1943, they took my friend's family to Auschwitz. She found out because even in Auschwitz the Czech Jews from Theresienstadt were kept for a while in a special camp. And they were made to write postcards about how well they were being treated there. . . .

The friends of her family received one of these . . . postcards. But they did not believe what was written. They knew it was a trick, and so did my friend. And, in fact, there was no more word from her parents or her little brother or her sister. They had all been taken to the gas.

My friend did not know exactly what happened. But she knew that her family was gone. This was already 1944, and almost all the Jews were gone. They were gone from Germany. They were gone from Czechoslovakia. Millions of Jews were gone from Poland.

(*steps forward to more fully engage audience*)

So my friend, she did a crazy thing. She herself does not know why she did it. Maybe it was despair. Maybe she no longer wanted to live. Maybe she really was crazy and did not know what she was doing. But she called the Gestapo headquarters. She just called them up on the telephone, the very people who were taking the Jews away. And when the Gestapo officer answered the phone and asked her what she wanted, she said she would like to report a missing person.

"And who is missing?" the Gestapo officer asked.

(*still amazed by the story*)

And my friend said that her mother was missing. She had been in Theresienstadt, and then she had been put on a train, and now she was missing. And then my friend said that her father was also missing. And her little sister. And her little brother.

She gave the Gestapo officer their names. Just as though it was normal circumstances. And then she described them for him, (*soft irony*) so he would know them if he found them.

(*strong, slow, crystalline*)

My mother has long, flowing, beautiful red hair. And freckles. My father is a strong, handsome man. He is tall. He used to play a lot of soccer. My little brother is eight years old. He has red hair and freckles like my mother. And my little sister is six. She is dark and strong like my father.

And the Gestapo officer took all the information. And apparently, he was very polite. He promised to call her back if he heard anything about the whereabouts of her family.

"And how can I get in touch with you?" he asked. And my friend told him where she lived. She told him the *truth*! And she told him where she worked and what she looked like. She told him more than he would ever need if they wanted to find her.

(*pause, very deliberate from this point on*)

But they never did find her. They never called. They never came. She never heard anything from them.

Maybe they assumed she was crazy.

Maybe they assumed she was already dead.

Dolls
(a woman)

All they did on Kristallnacht was decapitate my dolls. I had a wonderful collection. I was a little girl who loved all her dolls. And we were lucky. Somebody warned us they were coming. When we returned to the apartment, the dolls were sitting together, leaning against each other, on our dining table. And their heads were all cut off.

(*moves downstage to help with transition from horrific memory to genuine enthusiasm*)

My husband and I went back to my hometown in November '88. And we had a *wonderful* time. Truly! It was totally gemütlich. The people couldn't have been nicer. They were glad to see us. This was for the fiftieth anniversary of Kristallnacht. They invited all the Jews from my hometown who had survived.

(*No smirking through description of exhibit. Let audience find the irony as they do.*)

And they had an exhibit called *All the Jewish People Around the World*. With a big chart that looked just like my son's in our basement. His is called "Sea Mammals of the World"—all the seals and whales and porpoises and the places where they live. And my hometown had *All the Jewish People Around the World*.

The Israeli Jews wore little kibbutz hats. And the Russian Jews had violins. The American Jews had round and happy faces. And the Argentine Jews wore colorful clothes.

And dolls too. They were selling dolls too—"Jewish People Around the World" dolls. Just like the American Indian dolls we have in this country. In America. All dressed up in native clothes.

And a lovely little girl came running up to me. A German girl, from my hometown. And she had one of these dolls—a little blond German Jewish doll.

(*Leans over with hands out to cradle the received doll. A position she maintains until the end, when she uses her cradled hands to return the doll.*)

And she put it in my hands. And she said, "This is Elsie and she's Jewish and I love her." She put it right in my hands. To show me Elsie, and how much she loved her.

And my husband turned completely pale. I swear to God, he was absolutely white. He knows me well. He reads my mind.

(*maintaining tight control*)

But I didn't do anything. I just gave it back.

I did nothing at all. I just gave it back.

I didn't tear its head off.

How to Survive

(a man)

(*Big. This guy knows where he's going and how to play an audience.*)

Whenever I speak, someone ALWAYS asks me: "How did you survive?"

That's what they always want to know: How did I survive? What gave me the strength to go on? What gave me the hope to get through?

I don't know why they always ask this. Maybe because today *everybody* wants to be some kind of survivor.

(*enacts scanning bookstore shelves*)

Like, I go to the bookstore, and I look at the books. And they have *How to Survive the Loss of a Love*. And *The Survival Guide for New Parents*. Then they have *Surviving the Breakup* if you're going to get a divorce. And *The Stepfamily Survival Guide* if you're going to get together.

See, it doesn't matter if you're gaining people or you're losing them. It's survival either way! And everybody wants to be some kind of survivor.

(*confiding*)

So I was curious. I decided to read one of these survival books. This was Norman Cousins—you know, a Jewish guy—and he wrote *The Anatomy of an Illness*. Have you read it? It's about how he survived an illness.

You see, Norman Cousins, he got some kind of bad arthritis. In the meantime, he had a lousy doctor. So he gets another opinion, and he finds a doctor who lets him do whatever he wants. So what does he want to do? He takes a lot of vitamin C, and he watches a lot of funny movies, and he laughs—and eventually his arthritis goes away. He says that laughter and jokes give a big boost to the immune system. So, apparently, the immune system has a sense of humor . . .

(*If the audience is laughing, he has them where he wants them.*)

Anyway, Norman Cousins, he says, if you want to survive you should look at the bright side, watch the comedians, and find a doctor who's not a sourpuss. That's how Norman Cousins survived.

(*beginning of turn, he keeps smiling until he lands on "hatred"*)

I'll tell you, though, for me it was different. And what helped *me* survive, they don't write it in a book. It's not in any of the books that I looked at. And I don't think they're going to put it in *Reader's Digest* either. Because I don't think people really want to read this—

Because, you see, what helped *me* survive was not jokes and funny movies and looking at the bright side. No.

Not at all. What helped me survive was *hatred*. Pure, undiluted hatred. And the wish for revenge.

(*escalating rage*)

So when I was in the camp, and I looked at the SS man with the machine gun in the tower, I said to myself: "One day *I'm* going to have that machine gun. One day, *I'm* going to be up in that tower."

(*near hiss*) See this is the power of hatred. The power to stay alive—to stay alive (*looking up to remembered SS man*) because I looked at that SS (*slam it*) SONOFABITCH—

And I said to myself

(*full-bore rage, pointing at guard tower*)

I'm going to survive ***you***! I am going to survive ***you***! You will be torn to ***pieces***. And I will go on!

(*holds rage but clearly distressed by his loss of control*)

And thank God I did! Thank God I did! Sh'ma y'Israel! Thank God I did!

(*hold for four to five beats with fist up, head down, looking defeated rather than triumphant*)

The Vanity
(a woman)

Whenever I am introduced as a "survivor," I'm a little bit uncomfortable. I mean, what do people want? What do they expect?

In the beginning, until just the last few years, nobody wanted to hear from us. Everybody said, "This is to forget! Life goes on! Hush up your bad dreams!" Like—this may sound silly—but we heard in this country, "When you laugh, the whole world laughs with you. And when you cry, you cry alone."

So that's exactly what we did. We said, "We're Americans too." And we are. And we kept our memories to ourselves.

Now, today, everybody makes a big deal out of it. I mean, they don't just invite us to speak, but they turn us into some kind of heroes. They talk about the special wisdom we're supposed to have. And the precious legacy we're supposed to pass on. And all the tales and legends (*ironic*) *we're* supposed to be able to retell?

What is this, a bar mitzvah? A celebration of our Jewish roots? I mean, we, whose roots were totally destroyed, are supposed to have a precious legacy? And we, who can hardly speak at all, are supposed to tell you fabulous tales and legends? (*beat*)

In the beginning, people were silent. Today, they are stupid.

(*beat, transition to reassurance*)

But I'll tell you. I'm stupid too. I don't have wisdom. I don't even know what I think. I mean, I lived through it. I remember it. But even *I* don't know what the Holocaust means or what we should believe about it.

One memory I will tell you, because then maybe you will understand this stupidity of mine. You know, I was part of the time in Birkenau. Birkenau—that was the part of Auschwitz where they had the gas chambers. In the shower room. And the crematoria. Birkenau was where they killed most of the people in Auschwitz.

And I was in the group of prisoners who sorted the clothes of those who had already been gassed and burned. After they went into the shower room . . . the gas chamber . . . we came out and packed up the clothes they left behind.

And also in Birkenau there was the prisoners' latrine—you know, where we went to the toilet—which was really just a bench with a row of holes over a pit filled with quicklime. So this was where we went to the bathroom.

And in the latrine of Birkenau, the SS took one lady, one of the prisoners, and they made her the *Scheisskapo.*

This was a joke for the SS. It means, "the shit commander." That was her title. It was on a sign she wore around her neck. And her job was to watch the toilets and be like a kind of attendant. She had to keep it neat and clean.

And one day I noticed this lady, the *Scheisskapo*, had managed to find a few boxes. Somehow, she got a couple of old crates made of wood. And she put them together with the little one in front, so she could sit on it. And she also had a little mirror that she probably found in the clothes—from one of the prisoners who had been killed.

(*slowly bending knees to suggest sitting at vanity*)

So with the boxes, and the mirror, she made like a little bureau. She put the mirror over the big box, and she sat on the little box, and made like a little vanity in the corner of the latrine. A little vanity in the corner of the ladies' room.

(*two beats, stands up straight*)

Whenever people ask me, "What does the Holocaust mean?" Or I ask myself, "What does it mean?" I think about this memory. It's not easy to do. Try to keep the picture—all the elements of the picture—together in your mind at *one time*:

A vanity

In the latrine

In Auschwitz-Birkenau

(*beat*)

Now you tell me—you tell me, because I don't know myself.

(*Gradually widens arms; a real question, paces lines to keep audience with her every step of the way. Valence is neutral all the way through.*)

Does it inspire your hope

or your revulsion

that the attendant

in the toilets of Hell

made a place

to put on

her makeup?

(*arms now fully out, held for seven to eight beats, blackout*)

END OF PLAY

What Remains

Overview

I began the pieces that make up *What Remains* in 2021. Although it is written in a different voice than *REMNANTS*—my own looking back on a "life among survivors"—I intend it also to be spoken as well as read. And, indeed, I have presented parts of it in staged readings and spoken memoir workshops.

A fond hope is that some readers will read out loud parts of *What Remains*—as they also will of *REMNANTS*—not for public performance but as a second way into the text. Its arrangement on the page—especially the use of vertical spacing between the paragraphs or "beats" of each entry—is specifically intended to facilitate recitation. Even without knowing that, some readers of the manuscript told me that they spontaneously read sections out loud, which was, of course, gratifying to hear.

In my teaching, I often combine reading and reciting, including in class. As in transcribing, deep listening most reliably depends on *re*listening. When I teach with survivors' video testimony, I often have students "reverse engineer" portions of a video by creating a written transcript of a section in which I know there is much easily missed in a single watching. I am pleased that, in course evaluations, students often say that they learned as much about listening in general as about listening to survivors.

Still, listening—however long and deeply—is only part of what has mattered over decades of my conversations with survivors. At least as important has been the process of "learning together," in Agi's phrase. Learning together inherently requires two living people, revisiting earlier conversations in ways that often generate new memories, new insights, as well as refining (and sometimes undermining) earlier assumptions. Learning together also requires a candid and trusting relationship, which itself is as important an outcome as anything that results from it. I return to this point at the end of *What Remains*.

Here, it is enough to say that demography has caught up with what many told me—I'll describe the circumstances—when my work began almost fifty years ago: that "the survivors are all dying." Survivors *are* now dying in significant numbers. And, along with them, the chance to "learn together" with survivors also dies. There are no surrogates—interactive technology, survivors' heirs, or people like me who have spent much of their life with survivors—that can replace it. Some things end. "Learning together" with survivors is one of them.

What Remains follows a trajectory that begins with a piece called "Gone," which concerns some of these issues, and ends with a piece called "Returns," which suggests some of what can be carried forward—if not in our direct relationships with Holocaust survivors, then with others who have gone through hell and managed to come out the other side. Of course, there is much else that remains—memories of cherished relationships and conversations, treasured insights, gratitude for all of this, and the always present shadow of loss. These are not small things.

As in all my writing, my beloved Agi Rubin appears in many parts of *What Remains*. So also Abe, who is Manny from Mars in *REMNANTS*. Maria/Miriam (the double name will be explained) is the actor who performed "The Vanity" for the original radio production of *REMNANTS*. While we didn't know it when we cast her, she was herself a Holocaust survivor—then a child who survived, barely, by passing as a Polish Catholic and who was forced to move from place to place seeking protection. And there are survivors whose experiences are not represented in *REMNANTS* but with whom I learned things equally essential to crafting the play and to my work more widely.

While *What Remains* is written in my own voice, survivors' voices still play a key role. Recalling my relationships with survivors necessarily includes remembering things they said. There are profoundly, often ironically, humorous moments in these pieces. There are also moments of grief, futility, uncertainty, and almost otherworldly peace—survivors' and my own. There is much that I anticipate will be surprising. Like my favorite audience comment about *REMNANTS*, my own experiences with survivors were also often "not what I expected." I took that as a sign that we were getting somewhere.

What Remains

Gone

Most of the survivors I first met fifty years ago are gone. I'm not sure why I say "gone," as though they've only left. As though they might be back.

Sometimes I say, "they're no longer on the planet." As though they might be on another planet.

It's been hard to let them go. Not only for me. Even as it has also been hard to let them be among us. As though survivors actually were from another planet. I'll be saying more about that.

Beyond my family, being with survivors, schmoozing *with* survivors, thinking and writing *about* my schmoozing with survivors has been the center of my life. The cliché applies. Some really *were* family. We adopted each other. They were short on family because of the war. I was short on family, well, because of my family. That's a different story. For a different time.

Agi Rubin was the center of the center, the heart of all these years. For eight months in 1980, we met every Monday for an interview that became a conversation that became friendship that became a coauthored book. We met over coffee, cigarettes, and lunch—in various order. Agi was Hungarian, and she cooked like one. Paprikash. Paprikash. Paprikash.

I once gave an oral history talk called "Let There Be Lunch." The point was that people often say things over a meal that are rarely said in recorded interviews. For example, referring to her participation in one of the large video testimony projects, Agi said she gave them her "usual spiel": the default account when she was invited to "talk about the Holocaust." There is nothing unusual about this. We all have a repertoire of practiced accounts about important events in our lives. We learn what is tellable by us and at least relatively hearable by our listeners. We learn what works with different listeners and in different situations. Survivors do the same.

Over years of conversations, Agi and I didn't talk only about the war and survivors and listeners. We spoke about pretty much everything. We shared our lives. So whatever we discussed about the Holocaust emerged within a full relationship. Agi met all my girlfriends from those years. For reasons I'll never know, she often remembered one of them as "Diane." I never went out with a Diane. Perhaps I should have. Perhaps somewhere there is a Diane Paprikash.

Seders at Agi's were unique. The guests called themselves the Hungarian Mafia. Doctors, lawyers, dressmakers, shopkeepers. No gangsters as far as I know. They welcomed me even though I'm part Galitzianer, part Viennese, and maybe a little Litwak. They'd asked me. As is Passover tradition, they welcomed the stranger.

Agi was very pleased with, I'd say proud of, my reconstruction of her own memories in *REMNANTS*. "The Vanity," her story, is the anchor of the play. She came to many performances, both before and after I began doing it solo. One of the befores was a production by a well-known professional Jewish theater in Detroit. Like many Jewish theaters doing Holocaust-themed plays—and professional theaters in general—they went way over-the-top. If there's any topic that doesn't need over-the-top, it's the Holocaust. Less is more. Even less is even more. After the performance, Agi sidled up to me and whispered: "Never let them do it again." She took a step back and winked. "*Never again!*"

You have to be in the Mafia to say stuff like that.

In later years, when I heard Agi recount the experience that "The Vanity" recalls, I realized that she retold it increasingly like the version that is reconstructed in *REMNANTS*. I don't mean verbatim but closer to its pacing, connections, and conclusions. In essence, she was borrowing back *my* retelling of what I initially borrowed from her. Whoever was retelling it, "The Vanity" had developed between us.

I confess I felt both giddy and guilty when I first noticed this. Or maybe guilty over the giddy. Born in New York after the war, I had influenced a survivor's testimony? Even, in effect, cowrote some of it?

But then I realized that all the stories we tell, especially the most important, are cowritten in one way or another. They all develop between us. For example, when we share a memory with a friend, someone who knows us well, they may suggest a metaphor, connection, or theme that helps capture what we were trying to convey. And the next time we tell that story, we may well draw on our friend's metaphor, connection, or theme—without giving them a footnote! Footnotes are not needed. All that is needed is good conversation. And often good friends.

Once again, a process of "learning together" as Agi described it for me so long ago. She is there, in words and memories of words, in every class and everything I write—scholarly or dramatic. So is she "gone" or not? Like the end of "The Vanity," which is also the end of *REMNANTS*, I think this is a question best left unresolved. Meanwhile, irresolution also leads to good conversation as we work to sort it out.

Good conversation, "deep schmooze" as I often call it, is for me the goal of everything—whether with survivors, students, colleagues, people more generally. Deep schmooze will not solve the world. But it is hard to imagine anything without it that will.

In 2016, I received a voicemail from Agi. She was in the hospital, and she said that she needed my help. She said there was one more chapter we needed to write. It would be about all the people who had helped her through her life. It would be a chapter of gratitude.

The book that Agi and I coauthored had been published ten years earlier. Of course, I knew there was no possibility of adding a chapter. But logic, in such instances, is beside the point.

The next day I went to the hospital. Agi was dying of emphysema and barely able to breathe. She recognized me, but not much more. She didn't mention the chapter she had imagined the day before.

So this memory must itself represent a part of that chapter, that gratitude, which I return. From these fifty years of my life among survivors, Agi and others you will meet, gratitude is a large part of what remains.

The Auslander

In the late '90s, I presented *REMNANTS* at the new British Library in London. I had been invited to the UK to consult about a planned Holocaust exhibit at the Imperial War Museum. Doing the play was an add-on.

In truth, it was not a good performance. I was tired and distracted. Still, I had done it enough times to accept that it is never the same.

Nevertheless, I was surprised by the question of one audience member. Stretching out one syllable to the breaking point, she asked: "How much do they paaaay you to do this, this thing?"

It was clear in her phrasing—and the syllable that was a bridge to nowhere—that less than nothing would be too much. As luck would have it, "nothing" was the answer. My compensation in London was entirely for my work with the Museum and the British Library Sound Archive.

Withered as I was, I managed to respond with some version of, "Actually, I'm doing it for free." I wondered if "free" was a meaningful expression in English English. But I thought I saw a flicker of ironic satisfaction grace my interlocutor's face.

From there, it was mostly downhill, which suggests a bigger hill than it was.

I was restless and unhappy and, OK, angry when I got back to my hotel. I was frustrated that my hosts didn't come more to my aid. In fact, some had. They said nice things about my work and the piece. Some went out of their way to differentiate what I do from the project that was then simply called "Spielberg." To be "Spielberg" in that group, at least then, was not a good thing. And it was assumed that any American who did anything about the Holocaust must be a "Spielberg." I was just beginning to figure that out. In Israel, to be a "Spielberg" was even more damning.

I couldn't sleep. I considered calling Sid, my best friend and closest colleague. But it was after 3 a.m. in London, which meant after 10 p.m. in Detroit. And Sid was not a night guy.

Nevertheless, at 3:30, I cracked. Sid answered.

"Hello?"

He sounded asleep. I gave him perhaps three seconds to wake up.

"Sid. This is Hank."

"Hank?"

"Yes."

"Where are you?"

"London."

"London?"

"Yeah. England London."

"Oh yeah," he said. He recalled I was going.

By this point, I felt like a complete jerk for calling Sid at that hour.

"Sid, I feel like a complete jerk for calling you at this hour."

"Are you OK?"

"Yes . . . I mean, yes and no. Basically, yeah, I'm OK. I'm sorry."

"What's wrong?"

Sid was like that.

"Are you awake, I mean, enough; I mean . . ."

"Tell me."

"So, OK, I'll make it short."

That was a lie. I never make it short. Sid knew that.

"Some British survivor lady ran me through."

I am prone to overstatement.

"What happened?"

I told him the story, with appropriate timing, accent, and expression, including her extended syllable and my wilt.

Sid was quiet. Eventually, "It was good you were doing it for free."

"What?"

"I mean, that you could say that."

"Oh."

"She thinks you're Spielberg."

"Without the money."

"Right. Spielberg would not have done it for free. Malcolm told me he never pays for lunch."

Malcolm was a filmmaker and mutual acquaintance.

"Maybe that's a point in my favor? The free thing?"

I was searching.

I don't remember most of the rest of the conversation. It was not about the show anyway; just connecting with a friend. I apologized again for calling, but I was feeling much better.

"You'll find out more tomorrow. Something else is going on. That's what it sounds like."

Sid was the most generous person I've ever known and genuinely beloved by the survivors with whom he'd been working as long as I had. But he did not hesitate to confront a power-broker survivor in our area whom even other survivors called "der Führer." Behind his back.

With or without furor, survivors have often been wary of their would-be collaborators—whether psychologists, historians, or artists. This was particularly true in earlier years, when they and the Holocaust suddenly gained popular interest, after years of relative neglect. Many felt patronized or downright exploited. They were not entirely wrong.

In any case, Sid was right. I learned that while I was off resting and rehearsing before the performance, there had been a pitched battle between British historians and British survivors about whose voice mattered, who really knew anything about the Holocaust, and who should decide what would be in the Museum.

The battle continued into the next day. Positions hardened. People stopped speaking with each other. Stalemate.

For reasons still a mystery to me, I was asked to say a few words at the end of the last day to summarize the conference. Talk about going back into the breach. I think the idea was that, as an Auslander, the only non-Brit in attendance, I might have a semblance of neutrality. In any case, I had already been skewered and perhaps had nothing to lose. And I would soon be on a plane and far away. And since I was a psychologist, perhaps I could do something useful. And perhaps I was the only person they could think of.

Anyway, I could use redemption. But the odds of getting it seemed nonexistent. So, of course, I went for it.

The room was packed. Lady Macbeth and her entourage were sitting in the front row. I tried not to look at them.

I don't remember most of what I said. But I felt I got traction when I told the story of a similar project in Detroit. Then, too, a key number of the survivors did not trust others—especially academics—to get it right, even though they had invited some of us to work with them. They anticipated that both they and their experiences would be misrepresented. As *REMNANTS* suggests more than once, that certainly happens. There were weeks of push and pull until push won. The project broke apart. It dissolved.

I emphasized that simple fact. "Learning together" is a fine ideal, but it is also a fragile one. These collaborations are not easy. They can take enormous patience and effort. And they can easily fail. In Detroit, we *did* fail, despite the best efforts of many survivors and others. Failure is probably more common in such projects than success. That, I said, is reality.

I could tell that this last part, talking candidly about the real possibility, even likelihood, of failure had an impact. People stirred. A few questions were asked. Suggestions arose. They decided to keep talking. Which, an hour earlier, would have been a surprise.

I was obviously pleased. This was much better than a good performance. This had immediate practical impact.

I called Sid from the airport.

"Sid, you were right. The afternoon before the performance there had been a war between the survivors and the academics. I walked into it without knowing."

"Ah."

"But I may have helped things. At the last session, I told them the story of our experience in Detroit. Nobody there wanted things to fail. They started talking again. It may work out."

"So you're not a 'Spielberg' anymore?"

"Tony [one of our British colleagues] said I was a 'Clinton.' I schmoozed them back into schmoozing."

"Oy."

Sid and I started interviewing around the same time, and we became close with many of the same survivors. Whenever we were together—whether at our offices or at conferences, weddings, bar mitzvahs, family occasions of all kinds—we ended up in a corner having what we called "the conversation." It could easily go on for hours. Our families weren't thrilled. But we were obsessed, driven to share insights and reflections about the survivors we both knew. Without "the conversation," there is no possibility that I could have done the work I did, either as teacher or as writer.

I talk about my relationship with Sid in every class I teach about this topic. "Don't try to do this alone," I tell students. That's why we do it in class. That's why all of us need, if we are lucky, friends like Sid—people with whom we can journey, and learn, together.

We called each other brothers, emulating two survivor-friends—Abe and Alex—who also called each other brothers. The week Sid died of liver cancer, I brought over a bottle of Lagavulin, our favorite single malt scotch. He was weak but still fully awake. I remember pouring him a shot. "Well, Bro, at least you won't have to worry about your liver."

We were that kind of friends. And that's why I dedicate *What Remains* to the memory of Sid Bolkosky, my brother.

Crazy

In our first interview in 1980, Abe asks me: "So Hank, you're a psychologist?"

"Yeah," I answer. "I mean, I'm still in training."

"Training. OK. So, as a psychologist, still in training, do you think we're crazy? Do you think the survivors are all crazy?"

I tread water. Abe rescues me.

"*Of course, we're crazy.* You'd have to be crazy to go through something like that and not be crazy."

I love telling Abe stories. He was a hot dog, which had nothing to do with surviving the Holocaust. His stories from childhood, well before the war, were mostly about his standing up to "big shots." And how he likes to "*Aroys reden!*"

"You know Yiddish? You don't know Yiddish. *Aroys reden.* To speak out. *Aroys reden.* I'm not shy! Ask my wife! I'm not shy."

I didn't have to ask his wife.

Abe especially enjoyed visiting university classes.

"I was a little Jewish kid in Romania. And now you professors invite me to the big University of Michigan. So maybe I'm not such a little kid anymore!"

In a Holocaust history class—not my own—a student gets up and asks the most obsessively qualified question I'd ever heard:

"Uh, I was wondering, I mean, do you think, that the Roosevelt administration, possibly, well, that maybe they could have done more, I mean, during the war, if they had wanted to, during the war, that they could have done more, to, like some people say, do you think . . . ?"

Abe waves his hand to shut him up. Really, to put him, and the rest of us, out of misery.

"I can answer your question in three words. WE GOT SCREWED!"

As usual, he brought down the house. No one reads an audience better than Abe.

During our first meeting, Abe called another survivor to matchmake. "Zoli, there's this kid [I was thirty-two at the time] from the University of Michigan. He's interviewing survivors. Here, make an appointment."

Abe shoots me the phone. "Talk to Zoli. Set it up."

"Zoli? Look, I don't want to . . ."

Abe in the background: "Set it up!"

"I can call later. . . . You will? Sunday. At four? Sure. Great, great. Good. Sunday at four. 325 Maple. Great. Great. I'll see you then."

I pass the phone back to Abe.

"Zoli, he's a good kid, but he's a psychologist. So don't say anything."

Abe finishes the call, then back to me.

"Zoli is a good guy. You'll like him. He is also crazy."

Abe came to many *REMNANTS* performances, and he was not shy there either. "I'm Manny," he shares with audiences. "My cousin is the one with the newsreels. The one who said, 'I saw the newsreels. I don't want to hear a word about it!'" Often, he further recalled how it was:

So, so, what are we going to do? Ask the people for sympathy? NO! We had to adapt ourselves to the mainstream of the country. To make a new life. To fend for ourselves. Not just me. It's everybody. You come to a big country like this, you're a drop in the bucket . . . You have to survive! And, thank God, we did!

We have come to like outspoken, spirited survivors, even when they're going after us. My God, they can go through all that, and still . . . be spunky? Like Dr. Ruth.

But we weren't always so appreciative. In the survivors-are-all-crazy era, we had other expectations. Jack Goldman recalls:

I was always uncomfortable when people would expect me to be the emaciated, depressed survivor every minute of my day. "Oh, you look so well," they would say, surprised that a year after liberation I no longer weighed eighty pounds . . . And having a dull job, and loving music, I used to whistle or hum a tune, without even knowing what the tune was. And people would say, "How can you whistle after all you've gone through?" Such questions seemed so ridiculous to me.

In general, there are two options. Survivors are either damaged goods—guilty, ghostly, and, in current lingo, traumatized traumatized traumatized. Or they are celebrants of life, heroes of the human spirit, spunky.

Between those options—the pedestal or the consulting room—not much. But between those options is where most survivors actually live. Survivors have complex, many-sided lives. In general, we are not good at imagining complex, many-sided lives.

So survivors become "the thing." In the first months of the COVID-19 pandemic, the *New York Times* listed the names and occupations of the city's dead. For survivors, occupation was listed as "Holocaust survivor."

Agi once exclaimed: "I'm *not* a quote-unquote, capital *S*, 'Holocaust Survivor.' I mean, I survived. But I'm not *The* Survivor. I'm not a category. Not a thing. We have enough experience being categories."

Some years ago, I gave a talk about survivors at a small college. At the end, a young girl—maybe nine years old—came up with her dad. She said her class was going to visit our local Holocaust museum the following week. She wondered where, in the museum, could she find Agi.

I realized that this lovely kid assumed that Holocaust survivors *lived* in the Holocaust museum. They are part of the permanent exhibit. In effect, Holocaust artifacts. I found myself imagining survivors housed in dorms, adjacent to the museum. And every morning, they put on their survivor suits and took up their posts.

No. I didn't say anything like that to the nice kid. Nine-year-olds get a pass in my book. And the truth is that it's hard *not* to conflate survivors with the horror they lived through. During the first years I met with survivors, I often felt it. "My God. I am sitting with someone who was actually *there*." Even for me—someone who has spent years critically reflecting on others' responses to survivors—they were somehow larger than life. And perhaps, having passed through the destruction, somehow larger than death.

At the end of class, my students, without prompting, typically line up to hug a survivor who had joined us. I've asked why. "It's just something we can do," they usually say. "They were there. And now they're with us." There was nothing patronizing about it.

Even *young* kids sometimes do the same. I once did part of *REMNANTS* for a middle school in Superior, Wisconsin—home of the Vikings, the school mascot. As usual, I also spoke a lot about Agi. An eleven-year-old gave me a pocket watch that his grandfather had bought for him. It was a Timex, not expensive, but obviously precious to him. There was a picture of a locomotive engraved on the cover. He wanted me to give it to Agi for him. Extraordinary, little kid generosity.

I tried to dissuade him. Agi would appreciate that he even had the thought of giving his watch to her. When he was insistent, I suggested sharing as an option. I would bring it to her. Tell her about you. And then we would mail it back. With some resistance, he agreed to that resolution.

He then asked me what no one ever had: "What are Agi's hobbies?" A wonderful eleven-year-old's question. I was charmed, but I didn't think "smoking, poker, and schmoozing" was what to say to a kid at Central Middle School in Superior, Wisconsin. So I said, "music, holidays with family, cooking," which was equally true.

He smiled. He was satisfied. And I am forever grateful that he didn't ask, "How can she cook after all she's gone through?"

Takeaways

Some years ago, I performed *REMNANTS* in Minneapolis. My host—a very nice person—asked me what I hoped would be the "takeaway" for audiences.

I can be snarky. "I guess the 'takeaway' is that a lot of people were taken away."

I've come to believe that Holocaust survival does not simply mean still being alive at the end of the war. Holocaust survival means every minute that life persists under the killers' rule. What separates survivors and the dead is not the horror that people experienced. It is the amount of time before luck and chance ran out.

My relationships with survivors have never been separate from my relationships with the lost. They are the same people. Even though I will obviously never feel the loss as survivors do.

Some years ago, I performed *REMNANTS* alone in Auschwitz-Birkenau. I performed it to the wires. To the mud. To the scattered bricks of what once were barrack chimneys. The barracks themselves, made of wood, had mostly rotted away.

I performed it for *them*, which was crazy. Why would they want to hear a play about what they experienced? Still, in cemeteries, we say what we need to say.

I did some of the play in what had been the Terezin family camp, a subcamp of Birkenau where inmates of the Theresienstadt ghetto were sent in '43 and '44. As *REMNANTS* retells, they were made to write postcards about how well they were treated there. By the time the postcards were received, their writers had been killed.

When I finished my recital, it was hard to leave. It was physically hard to clamber under the wires. There was no obvious exit. But mainly, it was hard to leave them.

I kept looking back. I found myself saying, "Come with me." And I indulged the fantasy that they were now behind me, that we were leaving together. Grandiosity beyond measure, I fancied myself the Moses of Birkenau. Performing the ultimate takeaway.

Outside the fence, there was a posted Visitor's Map of Birkenau. And I realized that I had not actually been in the Terezin family camp. I was one subcamp over. Muddy rectangles all look the same.

In fact, I had been in the Zigeunerlager, the gypsy camp, where whole families were also imprisoned and, after a few months, gassed. Every Birkenau survivor

I know remembers the night when the gypsy camp was—that euphemism—"liquidated." And the screams and the screams and the screams.

So I had performed *REMNANTS* for the gypsies, the Roma, the Zigeunerlager. And I confess I asked myself, "What should I do? Should I go back to the Terezin family camp and do the play again?" Yeah, I had that thought. Yeah, I wasn't sure.

Eventually, I turned back to the Zigeunerlager. "You come too." I was a liberal Moses. A Moses of diversity and inclusion.

The next day, our group crossed into the Czech Republic and visited the site of Theresienstadt itself. I was invited—I did not know it was going to happen—to perform *REMNANTS* in the Attic Theatre of the Magdeburg barracks, a space used for performance during the Holocaust itself.

For an hour, I have the room to myself. I am alone but not alone. Children run through lines. Practice. Practice. Practice. The urgency of rehearsal. Most for death. Some for life.

I run my hands across the benches and the walls, which I need to touch. The surfaces that they had touched.

My performance itself was in a cloud. I told the audience about doing the play in Birkenau the day before. I said that the theater was more crowded than it seemed. The fifty or so people who were there—our group and some additional visitors—were not alone. I saw those who had been in the room before.

Every now and then, I have imagined that more crowded room at later performances of the play. But only occasionally. One can call on the dead too often and make unfair demands.

It is too easy to imagine that they're not really gone.

Human Remains

Once, my wife was stopped going through airport security and asked to open a blue velvet box she was carrying in her purse. "What are those?" the guy asks. "My husband's teeth," she answers. He waves her through as quickly as he can. (They were my baby teeth that my parents had saved in a blue velvet box.)

After her gallbladder was removed, my mother came home from the hospital with her gallstones in a small glass jar. As a kid, I'm fascinated by them. It's amazing that these pebbles were once inside my mother. And now they are sitting on her dressing table. And I, who was also once inside my mother, am looking at them.

Human remains.

As a kid, I read a lot about archaeology. Kid archaeology. Mummies, pyramids . . . In my bedroom, there was a slit in the back of a bookshelf that led to a mysterious space behind. I discover I can slip thin bits of paper through it. I once wrote a note: "Letter to future archaeologists. My name is Hank Greenspan. I live at 34 Cooper Road in White Plains, New York. I really hope you find this. Here, it is 1958." (I didn't know if AD would mean anything.) I put my message to future archaeologists in the slit. I hear it fall downward between the studs to an imagined moment in which it, and I, are discovered.

I often looked for arrowheads. Once, I actually found one, on an island on Lower Saranac Lake in the Adirondacks. Doing the math, I realized years later that Lower Saranac is where I would have been conceived. When I found the arrowhead, I didn't know that. I'm just thrilled to hold something that was held by someone else, maybe hundreds, maybe thousands of years before, maybe more. It was in his hands—I assumed it was a him—and now it is in mine.

Human remains.

Years ago, I had a lovely kid in my seminar on the Holocaust. She was smart, but her writing tended to go tangential. Usually, she noticed. I was reading one of her swervy essays in our kitchen. Suddenly, she catches herself and returns to the topic. She writes: "Anyways, back to the Holocaust." I share it with my wife.

Since then, over twenty years, when my wife or I suddenly change topics, we say: "Anyways, back to the Holocaust."

Three of my grandparents died before I was born. My father's mother lived until I was four and a half. I remember her apartment on New York's Upper West Side. I remember naps in a bed with a specific grandmother smell. After she died, my parents told me that her last words were "How's Hank?" I have no idea if that's true. I hope it is.

Henry Krystal, an Auschwitz survivor and a teacher of mine, once told me: "Part of what helped me survive was that I knew my mother loved me."

Human remains.

I understand that T.S. Eliot was an antisemite, although there's apparently some debate. Either way, like many, I'm drawn to this line from *The Waste Land*: "These fragments I have shored against my ruins."

Fragments, ruins. I know a Holocaust survivor who endured the Lodz ghetto and Auschwitz. Reuben owned a small electric parts store in what we used to call "inner city Detroit." He tells me that he could have moved his store after the 1967 Detroit riots, or rebellion, but he stayed.

I could have moved out years back. But sometimes, I just feel, I don't know—it reminds me sometimes, like, the buildings, you know, all boarded up. Sometimes it reminds me, like, like the ghetto. From the riots in the city. They never did nothing to it after that. Everything is boarded up. And ruined. It's a lot like in the ghetto. In Lodz.

After '67, only a few customers came. Reuben spent most of each day alone in his store, "dreaming back," as he says, to prewar Jewish Lodz. He even imagined writing a novel. "Not about the Holocaust, but about the *whole life, the whole life, the whole life*, before the Holocaust. With the Holocaust included."

Reuben never wrote the novel. I think he lived it: finding a ghetto that reminded him of *that* ghetto, choosing not to leave, shoring fragments from a whole life. Unpublished and unpublic, it was, indeed, a dream.

In Birkenau, Agi found a photo of a favorite cousin in her mother's jacket in a pile of clothes from those already gassed. She hid the photo in her shoe and kept it until liberation. By then, it was only white powder.

Human remains.

Agi also had a recurring dream in Auschwitz. She was a child cradled in her mother's lap. "But the fence, the barbed wire is there. And it always ends with that. The good, sheltered feeling is very temporary, it is very minor. That's how far you could go. Even in a dream."

After my sister, Carol, died at fifty-two, my wife and I traveled to Boston to "make arrangements." We picked out a gravesite. One could pretty much choose any plot in the new cemetery. And so my wife and I walk around, talking about the advantages of the "view" Carol would have (keeping in mind her horizontal plane) from this spot versus that one. "View" is important. Almost always, we imagine it is for them rather than for us. It is a way of shoring memories and care.

Human remains.

Baby teeth, gallstones, fragments of a photograph, fragments of a dream, a single plot chosen at twilight—these are small things compared with monuments, memorials, museums. . . .

I've come to believe that grief is a piecemeal business, tangible, specific. We can grieve a single person we love and for whom we carefully choose a grave. But I don't think we can grieve the *whole life* of a people, mostly without graves; for us, mostly without names.

Agi told me that a friend of hers, another survivor, asked if she could visit Agi's father's grave as a place to grieve her own father, lost in the flames. Agi's father survived the war so there *was* an actual grave. The friend said she'd asked her rabbi, who said it was OK. Agi said, "Of course, it's OK."

Human remains.

I was with Agi when the United States Holocaust Memorial Museum opened in '93. A cold, wet, brutally windy day. The Mall, stretching out behind the new museum, was a field of mud. Agi remembers:

For years I saw my mother floating in the air, in the smoke, in the wind, and I couldn't reach her. I couldn't bring her down . . . We want to feel that our dead are somewhere, and what happened to them is somewhere, and not simply erased . . . We want to believe that the museum is a place to remember, even a grave, even a cemetery. But I must tell you that this is improvisation, this is pretending, and we know it. We want to believe it, even as we are reminded that it is cold and it is raining and the wind still blows.

We can improvise. We can borrow one grave to stand in for another. We can borrow a ghetto in Detroit to stand in for the obliterated ghetto of Lodz. We can borrow a museum to stand in for cemeteries that exist nowhere. But there are limits. "That's as far as you can go. Even in a dream."

Agi's mother improvised during the first moments of their arrival in Auschwitz. Agi was sent to one side, her mother and little brother to the other. Agi ran over to be with them. But the SS shoved her back, pushing her to the ground.

Her mother saw this happening, even as her own line was led away.

"Go my child, go. We will see each other tomorrow."

Agi says, "And I have been going ever since then."

Human remains.

These days, there is endless talk about survivors' "legacies," which almost always means their testimony about what they witnessed and endured. Not so for Agi.

What is that word they always use? That word. That word . . . "Legacy. Legacy." What is my "legacy"?

We who were there know how limited can be any parent's ability to prepare the younger generation for what can happen. . . .

But then I think of my own parents, the legacy that I myself received. And I realize it is made up of small things that turned out to be precious to me: things that I gathered up as much because I needed them as because my parents wanted me to have them.

I barely remember my mother's face. But I somehow remember her principles, certain ways one tries to live one's life . . .

My father, who survived, was with me through much more of my life. It was a full, mature relationship. And yet, when I think of him, I remember certain moments. I remember the way he sang "En Kelohenu," one of our Jewish prayers. Whenever I am at the synagogue, I hear his voice. At certain prayers or hymns, I remember how much joy he got out of singing that particular one. And when it comes up, he is again with me, and I am singing with him. It is the harmony of voices that makes the legacy; the way I tune myself to him and feel his spirit singing through my own voice. Even now, we are singing together.

So, actually, what is a "legacy"? It's these small things that are taken up by those who follow. I can provide whatever I can provide. But, in the end, my legacy is not up to me. It is up to whoever comes after, to pick up this bit, remember that part, find harmony with whatever note, as it may apply to their own circumstances, which I know will be different from mine. You will take what you choose, what you need, just as I did. I can only wish you well and wish you peace.

So one last time, I remember my mother's voice. And I repeat what she said to me, as she looked across the mud and the agony, trying to get my attention, trying to imagine a future, trying to invoke hope, trying to bestow the only blessing that, in the end, this world allows.

"Go, my child, go."

Go my beloved children and grandchildren. Go my dear comrades and friends. Go, my kind listeners.

Go.

Maria Dying

I first met Maria as a voice in an audition audiotape for the radio production of *REMNANTS*. My codirector and I knew we had found the actor for "The Vanity," the final monologue of the play.

We didn't know when we received Maria's recording—she didn't say—that Maria was herself a Holocaust survivor. But by then, I had spent two decades listening to survivors. I sensed it. Her Polish accent; her audition recording of a Warsaw ghetto poem; something in her voice. Each syllable seemed chiseled from some larger block. She wanted more than a part in a play.

"I survived the war as a Jewish child in Poland." She told me this, but not much more, when we first met. I remember thinking it might be odd for a survivor to take the role of another survivor. Was there such a thing as *too much* authenticity? She added, "I am also an actor." We wanted her. Whatever she said would have been enough.

Never in a camp as Agi was, Maria was one of those we now call "hidden children." Passing as a Polish Catholic child, she moved from place to place, sometimes treated well, sometimes abused. Her name became "Maria" rather than "Miriam." As a nine-year-old, she came to believe in a Christ who would protect her. She became devout. In one of her hiding places, there was a crucifix in a pasture where she watched over cows. She enjoyed their company, and she prayed to a Jesus who, she believed, watched over her.

Every morning while taking the cow to the pasture, I walked past a small figure of Christ carved in wood. Standing on a crossroad, on a wooden pole, the figure also seemed lonely. Brown, weathered, cut in wood, he seemed to listen and understand. His bent figure expressed compassion. His small face looked at me approvingly.

While she had been going to church, she was able to pretend to take communion without anyone noticing that she hadn't really done it. She yearned to be genuine. Under the gaze of wooden Jesus, she decided it was time to tell the priest the truth. She would confess she had never been baptized but desperately wanted to be. She was pure in her faith. He would give absolution. And she would be free to take communion like the others.

But when, in confession, Maria told the priest she was not baptized—which could only mean she was Jewish—he refused absolution and forbade communion. He ignored her appeal. She returned to pretending, assuming no one would notice. But the woman who had knelt behind her at confession overheard the priest's verdict. And as Maria approached the pulpit, she screamed loud enough for everyone in the church to hear, "Father, this girl did not receive absolution."

Maria ran from the church and into the forest, where she spent the night. She imagined the woman's scream echo among the trees. "This girl did not receive absolution." Hiding in the underbrush if she heard someone coming, or thought she did, she feared they would kill her or turn her over to the Germans. Neither was unrealistic. "This girl did not receive absolution." She finally arrived at another farm where she'd heard she might find shelter.

When we speak of hidden children, "hidden" is usually a euphemism. The reality is more uncertain, precarious. Maria remembered:

As I moved from village to village, my days were alike. At daybreak I took Lyska, the cow, to graze. Mute, dumb, silent, I spent all my time with the cow.

Once, on a hot day, gadflies attacked Lyska in a pasture . . . Lyska's hide was covered with dark, grayish, stinging gadflies. She raised her head, wailing loudly. She bolted and raced toward the barn.

*That night . . . I dreamed that someone had discovered my secret. I wanted to run away, but my legs wouldn't move. I wanted to scream but couldn't utter a sound.**

Under attack, Lyska could wail and run. Maria was frozen and muted. One of my students once asked her if she'd wanted to be the cow.

Maria smiled. She was silent for a moment. And then she said, "Thank you."

After the war, Maria stayed in Poland. She might have stayed forever were it not for the antisemitic purge of '67, part of the Soviet Bloc's response to Israel's victory over their Arab allies in the Six-Day War. Maria studied and taught theater, to which she was devoted. She married a Polish Catholic man sympathetic to Jews. They had two young sons. She was still named Maria.

The government-owned press continued an anti-Jewish campaign. Every day I read articles condemning Jews.

She was tested by a supervisor, a government informer, at the school where she taught. He did not know for

* From Miriam Winter, *Trains* (Kelton Press, 1997), 91–92.

sure that she was Jewish. To her own surprise, she openly said that she was.

Write a letter to the newspaper condemning the Jews, and you can stay in your job.

She refused. "This girl did not receive absolution." She didn't ask for it.

Maria and her family left Poland forever.

With me, Maria shared the overview of her story early on. The more personal part came out only after years. It's tempting to invoke a cliché about hidden children: that they have gotten so used to hiding that they never fully emerge. But, of course, the same could be said of many of us. Whatever the reasons, Maria was often tense, tightly wound, when not engaged in a specific task—making a meal, a garden, or a play. I can't not notice that "wound" and "wound" are the same word. Over the years, I learned that her marriage was deeply wounded. So also her relationship with one of her sons. She moved through life with the discipline of a dancer—controlled, deliberate, precise.

All of this bears on Maria's dying, which I will recall. But that was in 2014, twenty-five years after the audition. Over those years, she wrote a memoir in which she reclaimed her Judaism and her identity as Miriam. She visited my class many times. She performed "The Vanity" on radio and stage, and her performance remains the gold standard for that monologue. When I began doing *REMNANTS* myself in the late '90s, I followed a lot of the tracks, including a light Polish accent, that Maria laid down. I call it the "karaoke school of acting."

I never got used to calling her Miriam rather than Maria. She understood that. When she left a message, she often used both names. "Hello, Hank. This is Maria/Miriam." I learned she did this with many friends. She was patient with us.

She was patient with us, but not so much with herself. Her meetings with my class were always successful. My students loved her. Still, she usually left unsure of how it had gone and asked my opinion. "Insecurity" is too small a word for a deeper uncertainty. She had told me that one result of the war was that she had lost much of her capacity to feel, at least spontaneously. She blamed that for the problems with one of her sons. She could not mother in the way she wanted. It seemed to her that he could not forgive her, and she could not forgive herself. Since the war, something remained frozen.

I recall one evening when she was with my wife and me after a performance. For no apparent reason, Nancy's knees suddenly buckled, and she fell to the floor. I called 911, and she was rushed to the hospital. The tests showed nothing of concern. It was most likely a blood pressure drop caused by dehydration. Maria stood on the other side of the room, watching the two of us with no reaction. No movement. No change of expression. As though nothing had happened. I thought about her son. And I confess I felt a chill. And a borrowed loneliness.

In the 2010s, Maria/Miriam was diagnosed with lung cancer. Early on, chemo seemed to be effective. Scans looked better. She looked better. There was a hint of remission. And then progression beyond the possibility of cure.

Maria sent me a poem.

Now That I Know*

The cardinal at my window saw
a red oak on the other side of the house
and plunged into the glass.

Startled, I watched this bird
short necked, reddish, pointed
bill hitting the window.
He flew away, swooped back, hit
with a force unexpected in such a small bird.

I watched him looping back
bright in the midday sun.

---

* Used with permission of David Orlowski, Maria/Miriam's son. Sadly, the poem was never accepted for publication elsewhere.

I too ran amok blindly
flapping my wings.
I kept hitting, relentless
eyes closed, head down.

Now that I know I have cancer
I watch the sand in my hourglass.

I soften my voice
put away the knives
wait for white arugula flowers
to bloom on my deck.
I want the hour to last
taste the sting on my tongue,
inside my cheek. Wind moves the chimes
on my neighbor's deck

Red cardinal listens.

Maria/Miriam mailed me the poem in March 2014. We had dinner a month later. In July, she died.

I visited her in hospice on what turned out to be her last full day. I thanked her for all she'd given—as a friend, an actor, a fellow teacher in my class. She reciprocated, recalling learning with my students, being in *REMNANTS*, what we'd shared over the years.

I've never had what I'd call a mystical experience. But those twenty minutes were the closest. And none of it was like anything I expected.

Maria (I now have to call her by the name most authentic for me) was glowing. I mean that literally. There was a warm, yellow-white light infusing the room. I didn't only see it, I felt it. Palpably. Viscerally. A sensory immersion in something I cannot name. I am tempted to write "communion," the converse of the one desecrated years earlier in Poland. And the opposite of frozen.

In truth, I have no idea what happened that day. "Putting away the knives," the relentless cardinal becoming the listening one, probably has something to do with it. But, at least for me, what I witnessed went beyond surrender or acceptance. Perhaps Maria knew what it was, but she can't tell us. I wonder if trying to explain moments like this may itself be a kind of desecration.

What I do know is that the feeling was still with me as I drove home. Rather than sad, I felt comforted, uplifted, serene. That lasted a few hours before fading. But the memory remains vivid.

I have been with a number of survivors at or near the end. Each meets death differently, which should be no surprise. Some, like Maria, seem to find an unexpected and extraordinary peace. Some, like Agi, are overcome with gratitude. Some struggle with bitterness.

Recently, I reviewed an article about survivors' final days. It argues that many cannot accept that the strength that got them through the war was not enough to save them from debilitating illness. Some associate being hospitalized with being locked away from the world, as they were in camps or in hiding.

I've heard versions of what the manuscript suggests. But far more typical among the survivors I've known is that, near death, their concerns are not primarily about themselves. Rather, they think about the lost, their "dear ones" as Agi always said—rarely with guilt—but with gratitude, longing, and sometimes ferocious loyalty. While popular rhetoric about survivors focuses on the future—survivors' legacies, next generations, useful lessons in resistance and resilience—survivors themselves think more about the past. To the extent they speak about those who will follow, it is with hope mixed with doubt mixed with the knowledge that whatever happens is both beyond their control and beyond their responsibility. Dying survivors—perhaps like most of us—return to their foundations: the people, the life, the world to which they once belonged.

And, in the best cases, the world where they were most unambiguously cherished.

Maria ends her memoir with a reflection about the ways and reasons she teaches theater.

Teaching acting in a small Midwestern town, I bring odd objects to class. My students find their true selves through tactile and sensual experience . . . Blindfolded, they open their senses; they touch, they smell, they hear. We walk through my garden, smelling herbs. "I remember eating pizza during a trip to Petoskey," someone whispers, holding a green sprig of oregano. Sometimes during a walk, bits of my own past turn up unexpectedly.

During the war, I cast off my senses. Hungry and cold, I learned to ignore my body as if it did not exist . . . I ignored my needs for rest, for shelter, and for comfort . . . I turned away from my body. Deprivation made me rigid and tense.

It wasn't until much later in my life that I began to learn again how to feel. Then, still later, I wanted to recall my past, but I couldn't. So I asked my feelings to teach me how to remember. I began by asking questions. "How does it feel to touch a fur collar? . . . How does my body respond to cold?"

Then I remembered the warmth of fire and fur. I remembered returning to the warm corner of a room, the oven still hot after bread making; fire, warmth, burning wood; the smell of cooked cabbage . . . [To] recover the smells of the time with my parents I have to recall czulent.

Czulent . . . baked in a red enamel pot. A dish of mostly potatoes and beef, baked overnight in a slow oven. Czulent is the sum and substance of my lost childhood . . . On Saturday morning the smell of czulent filled our small rented room in Ozarow, before I left home forever . . .

*I've never eaten such czulent again. I miss its taste. I miss the feeling on my tongue, on my lips, inside my mouth . . . I feel my lips touch the course, hard outer shell of a peeled potato . . . I bite into this single small peeled potato . . . The hard baked outer skin and the soft baked inner texture warm my mouth. I close my eyes, trying to recall the face of my mother.**

Perhaps it was Jesus who came to Maria on her last day. Perhaps it was *czulent*.

* Winter, *Trains*, 216–17.

Empty Rooms

A year ago, I was in the hospital and then rehab for almost a month. I had had serious illness in the past, including sepsis. But I never experienced what I did this time.

Looking at the ceiling from my hospital bed, I closed my eyes and saw an entirely different ceiling. Instead of white tiles, there was a textured brown surface—the kind of ceiling that would have been popular in the 1930s and '40s. I was not delirious or delusional. When I opened my eyes, I was back in the hospital room. The television on the wall, the reclining chair, the IV pole—everything just as it had been.

Where did this other, older ceiling come from? It didn't resemble anything I remembered. When I closed my eyes again, I saw an office from the same era—dark, wooden furniture, wood paneling, a large wooden chair and desk where business would have been done. It was a beautiful room, elegant, polished, everything in its place. When I opened my eyes, I was immediately back in my hospital bed, looking up. Nothing had changed.

The pattern continued. Closing my eyes, I saw carpeting that looked mid-twentieth century. Opening them, I saw the walls and floor of my hospital room. I could travel back and forth at will. I saw ornate lamps and other furnishings. Dark foyers. Fixtures for guests to hang their coats.

I knew I was in the hospital. I felt my weight in the bed. I heard the on and off of call buttons. Even while I could close my eyes and visit other rooms.

And then I realized the most important thing. All the rooms had no one inside. The people were gone. Disappeared. Absent.

Having taught and written about the Holocaust for fifty years, I thought I knew where I was "visiting." Empty European rooms where people used to be. I cried.

I cried, I think, because being close to my own death provoked this gallery. A gallery of "missing persons," a title from *REMNANTS*. The people were, indeed, missing. Notwithstanding the films and photos I had seen of prewar Jewish life, the empty rooms made the loss immediate. And irreparable.

Popular Holocaust memory has moved away from loss and grief. Remembrance observances may touch on loss, but, in general, they are relentlessly forward-looking. The rhetoric features resilience, resistance, hope, the future and its generations. Some museums have entirely dropped the word "memorial."

Where I live, the former Holocaust Memorial Center is now simply the Holocaust Center, preceded by the name of the steel company that is its biggest donor.

The deletion of "memorial" is related to the changing ways we've engaged survivors. At an earlier time, survivors were conflated with death itself. As many of the survivors I've known recalled, the newsreel images of liberated camps—skeletal figures immersed in a sea of corpses—made it hard to imagine that the same people could *have* a life after. "How can you whistle after all you've gone through?" as Jack Goldman remembers. When I first proposed a doctoral dissertation about survivors, the first three professors I approached said the same thing, almost verbatim: "Hank, the survivors are all dying. You should work with people who will be around for a while."

"The survivors are all dying." The profs told me that in 1975.

In 1975, fifty years ago, most of the survivors with whom I was already working were themselves around fifty—some a little older, some younger. None appeared to be on the edge of demise.

In the early 1980s, the rhetoric flipped. In the years of downsizing, shutdowns, and Bee Gees tryin' to "stay alive," being a "survivor" of *everything* took on unprecedented cachet, a development not lost on the wit industry. A 1979 *New Yorker* cartoon depicted two guys marooned on a desert island, one palm tree between them. While one appears glum, the other exclaims with enthusiasm: "That's what we are all right—survivors! People will say, 'Hey, those two are real survivors! Talk about survivors—look at those two!' Yes sirreee, no doubt about it, when it comes to survivors, we really. . . ." That the *New Yorker* published the cartoon (or "drawing" as they prefer) is proof enough that readers would get the joke. To draw from *REMNANTS*, "Everyone wants to be some kinda survivor!"

Holocaust survivors are "real survivors," apex survivors. Not surprising that, in popular imagination, they went from ghosts to celebrities, from damaged goods to men and women of exemplary wisdom and resilience.

A television commentator at the first World Gathering of Holocaust Survivors, held in Jerusalem in 1981, introduced his coverage:

These heroic people who are gathered here today have not come to resurrect the nightmares of the past. They have not come to mourn. They have come to celebrate life. To bear witness and to pass it on to their children and their children's children. This is more valuable than all the material assets they could pass on. This is their true legacy.

I spoke, well I cursed, back to the TV: "How is it possible to 'bear witness' without resurrecting the 'nightmares of the past'? Witness to *what*? And how is it possible to 'bear witness' to mass murder—often of one's whole family—without mourning, without grief?"

Some survivors have responded to the deletion of memorial and of grief. In 1981, the same year as the World Gathering, Sally Grubman reflected:

American Jewish teachers invite me into their classrooms to speak, but they do not want me to make the Holocaust a sad experience. . . . There is this book they use. The Holocaust: A History of Courage and Resistance, *but the Holocaust was never a history of courage and resistance. It was a destruction by fire of innocent people, and it's not right to make it something it never was.*

We are not heroes. We survived by some fluke that we do not ourselves understand. And people have said, "Sally, tell the children about the joy of survival." And I can see that they don't understand it at all. . . . We went through fire and ashes and whole families were destroyed. And we are left. How can we talk about the joy of survival?

It's not simple. In the same hours that Reuben told me about the world that was lost forever—and that he himself was a "lost soul"—a large mama sheep dog padded through the kitchen where we were talking, followed by six or seven rambunctious pups. The sound of his five kids coming and going was always in the background. Friends phoned constantly. He clearly was not, as he once suggested, simply a "ghost." However shadowed, here was also a "whole life."

When Abe exclaimed, "Of course, we're crazy! You'd have to be crazy to go through something like that and not be crazy!" he was not only doing shtick for me (although he partly was). He also told me about days when his "inner Nazis," as he called them, got the upper hand. He became anxious about losing everything—his business, his family, the life he created after the war. There was no obvious danger at these times. In that sense, he was "out of touch with reality." But he was certainly not out of touch in general. Losing everything was precisely what happened, to him as to so many others. It would be truly crazy *not* to imagine it happening again. This is not about memory. It is about knowledge—in the bones, knowledge.

So, again, complexity. Not one thing. Or the other thing. But many things, all at once. There is no higher synthesis. It doesn't add up. As survivors' listeners, we should allow things not to add up. Once again, Agi:

We survivors are bundles of contradictions. When we are here, we are also there . . . A smell, a sound, a feeling may be all it takes to bring it back. And even the past is split in two—memories of home, which we usually try to recapture, and memories of the destruction of home, which we usually try to forget.

So there are many strands at once. One world reminds us of the other; one thought leads to the next, and into the past . . . It is not that our joys are not real. They are entirely real. It is just that they never exist simply by themselves. They are always in reference to something else, something that can consume them in an instant.

*And then there are simply the blank spaces. The spaces where things were that are not anymore. Even when home and life are recreated, the losses are never made whole.**

"The spaces where things were." The spaces where people were. Perhaps that is where I visited that day in the hospital.

Empty rooms are also part of what remains.

---

* From Agi Rubin and Henry Greenspan, *Reflections: Auschwitz, Memory, and a Life Recreated* (Paragon House, 2006), 105–6.

Returns

I am surprised by how much *What Remains* is about loss. Given its title, that is itself a surprise. Still, I didn't anticipate how much memory and memorial would be, for me, inseparable.

After hearing from the profs in 1975 that "the survivors are all dying," I pushed against imagining the loss of "my own" survivors. I indulged the fantasy that at least some of them would never be gone. And I would not lose them.

Part of my preoccupation with loss also reflects the multiple catastrophes of our own time. I have often been asked what I thought Holocaust memory would be like in two decades, five decades, a hundred years. Along with the ways historical memory always changes, I've typically said some version of "it will partly depend on what else happens." There is no need to list contemporary disasters. I believe that more than one "what else" is already underway.

I've believed that for several years. So it is not surprising that my current play is not about survivors but about those who did not survive—and knew they wouldn't. The main character is based on an actual historical figure: Rubinstein (we don't know his first name) who was known as the "Mad Jester of the Warsaw Ghetto." Rubinstein's goal is not to prevent the destruction, which he does not believe is possible, but to ease our passage to it, through creative play (he was a street artist), imagination, and—above all—moving into our fate together. This from the opening monologue:

I am Rubinstein, the Mad Jester of the Warsaw Ghetto.

And I, Rubinstein, am also the undertaker of the Warsaw ghetto.

I play with *death.*

I play in spite of *death.*

I pretend we can still pretend.

I play.

I play the undertaker of the Warsaw ghetto.

Rubinstein is not talking about death in any ordinary sense. He is responding to the destruction of a people, of a "whole life" as Reuben emphasized, mostly without graves or names. He is talking about erasure, extinction, in which, as depicted in *REMNANTS*, even the remains of cemeteries do not remain. They are pulverized.

When Rubinstein speaks of pretending, therefore, it is pretending there could still be some version of normal loss and normal grief, even there. One of his antics was jumping into funeral carts and schmoozing with the corpses. At one point, he faked his own death in order to provoke a fake funeral, which was still possible in 1941. If only in memory, he aims to remind people—as I aim as playwright—that the lost are much more than how they were treated: as disposable nothing. Rubinstein's is a fool's errand, but that's what fools do. In a later scene, he says:

Without imagining, there is only the shit in front of you. By '42, only death . . . In '41, most people still imagined surviving. There might be a future. By the middle of '42, everyone knew it was over . . . So I was preparing them for the end. The corpses on the street were all of us. In waiting. But if you talk with the dead, joke with them, embrace them, they're not rubbish. Which means none of us are rubbish. That's what an undertaker does. It's a good show. Even if just for a moment.

No path leads directly from normal mortality to death within genocide. But the very difference, if one is aware of it, is informing. Strange as it may sound, death as many of us experience it is a privilege. Possibly an increasingly precarious one.

So it is a privilege to experience things like this:

I am moved, and sometimes unsettled, by the reality of generations. I used to think of academic conferences, which I still sometimes attend, as something like high school reunions. A chance to see old friends whom I have known for decades. But, unlike high school reunions, my own class is decreasingly represented. The conferences are full of younger scholars, many doing great work, but whom I rarely know. Someone offers me a chair.

Although formally retired, I still have students, including young ones, with whom I work online. Some say they want to "study with" me, which provokes the fantasy that I am a Yo-Yo Ma of Holocaust studies. Such students are at the other end of life, not much younger than I was when I first began my conversations with survivors. I see my midcareer colleagues raising families and establishing their own horizons of ambition. In general, they are full of the kind of fervor that once filled me.

Above all, I think about the survivors. And the extraordinary coincidence of coming up at a time when they, in ever greater numbers, were willing and wanting to talk at length with someone like me. When people hear about this, they sometimes thank me "for my work." As though I were in the army. I get that. But what is harder to understand from the outside is that these conversations—most essentially, these relationships—were the privilege of my life. It is still amazing to me that I got to do it. And that—as teacher, scholar, and playwright/actor—I got to share some of what I heard during all these years.

Those who have engaged survivors almost always emphasize what comes out of those encounters. Despite my questioning "takeaways," I have assembled my own collection. For example, survivors' perceptions of our perceptions of them. *REMNANTS* is as much about us as it is about survivors, especially the ways we represent them: as bestowers of legacies, psychiatric casualties, exemplary heroes, even "survivor" itself—which, Agi insisted, was a "thing" that she was *not*.

I have also focused on how survivors retell—their choices about what to share, when, and with whom. And what motivates those choices. Among the survivors I've known over decades, every one of them has told me that there are Holocaust memories they have chosen *never* to share, not with me or with anyone else. Notwithstanding the large testimony projects that now exist, the majority of survivors have not shared *any* of their experiences, except perhaps with other survivors. The "age of testimony" or "era of the witness," as academics like to call it, never involved more than a fraction of Holocaust survivors.

Typically, we assume that what is not retold has something to do with trauma or the otherwise emotionally unbearable. In fact, that is only rarely the case. For example, not telling may reflect protecting the memory of those who betrayed other prisoners. Survivors may not retell moments of exhilaration—even within the terror—which they assume, probably rightly, others will not understand. Not telling may simply reflect not telling, an expression of agency and choice. Either way, what will never be told by survivors is also part of what remains. So is the much larger silence of what will never be told by the dead.

Still, I have learned a great deal from survivors—about the unsaid as well as the shared. Over these fifty years, they have been among my most important teachers and closest friends. But the relationships in which we have learned together have never been only a means to an end. Those relationships have been equally the end itself. The necessary and sufficient reason to listen to survivors is to listen to survivors, just as it is to listen to anyone who has gone through hell and come out the other side. No "takeaway" is needed.

Although not represented in *REMNANTS*—he is in another play of mine—I end these reflections with a moment from my conversations with Victor. Victor was one of a handful of people who escaped from Treblinka and survived the war hiding in Polish forests. He was aware of the uniqueness of his story, even though he almost never retold it, and certainly not publicly. By his choice, Victor and I met in a location he disclosed to no one. Even his family did not know we were meeting. He lived in a world of secrets, betrayal, and exploitation—potentially by everyone. Without apparent bitterness, he shared:

Since the Holocaust I see a lot of races that are destroyed. The weaker has to give under, and the stronger survives. It is the law of the jungle, even by man. This is a world of circumstances. The ant, the rat, the cow, the horse, and the man—this is a world of circumstances.

For Victor, the same Darwinian circumstances, and outcome, characterized families, including his own.

An old man, full of wrinkles on his face, he is something surplus. Even to his closest, he is something surplus. He is useless. He starts to become a burden. To his closest. That's life. That's part of life.

It turns out that Victor holds far more complex and conflicting conclusions and emotions than these bits suggest. In the '90s, I was compelled to write two long chapters—a third of a book—trying to sort all this out. I did that, in part, because I knew how easy it would be to caricature Victor as one more bitter or guilty or whacked-out survivor. I could not change his fate.

But I thought I might at least take the fight to the caricaturists. And there is this: I realized sometime along the way that he reminded me of my father. Not his views, but his secrets and mystery.

In any case, I was not initially surprised when Victor foresaw the possibility that I, too, could betray him, mainly by exploiting his story for personal gain. He was not against my using what he shared. He only wanted to be sure that if I did so, and there was profit, he would get his share.

That's not unreasonable. But I did not think that there was any chance that the scholarly book I anticipated would make money. Still, I was glad to sign any contract that met his concerns. I drafted a few. He always dodged the issue.

In our last interview after a year of meeting intensively almost weekly and knowing we might not meet again, I asked him once more about a contract. Victor brushed my question aside, and he said this. It epitomizes what I have aspired to do over fifty years of sustained conversations with survivors:

You study me, and I study you. You study me with sharp eyes. I study you with dull eyes, through eyeglasses, but I can see that you go in with a sharp mind and sharp eyes. You look at me with eyes that want to find out what is behind my own eyes. I appraise it. I value it. I am thinking of it. I try to answer with what is of the heart. And you store it. You remember it. I only make the parallel, the connection between one individual and the other. It is good.

Obviously, I was honored by Victor's comment. But I repeat it here to suggest that "making the connection between one individual and the other" is perhaps the closest we come to remnants, awakenings, returns.

With Holocaust survivors as with everyone else.

Acknowledgments

So many people who made so much difference over so many years. There are too many to name: survivors, friends, teachers, colleagues, students, readers, actors, directors. The categories overlap so that the same person could easily be within several. And some, many, are gone. Which, of course, also goes with so many years. I do not distinguish here between the living and the dead. As Agi and perhaps Rubinstein might say, we are singing together either way.

Among those who helped me in the first years I began my conversations with survivors, I remember Professor Kurt Woolf, my dissertation chair at Brandeis, who read and commented on every page, almost every sentence, that I wrote. And Professor George Rosenwald at the University of Michigan who taught me much that I know about interview-based work. It is no accident that both Kurt and George were themselves émigrés from Austria before the Anschluss. I believe it is also no accident that they were as engaged in the arts as in scholarship—Kurt in poetry, George in music.

And there is an inner circle of both friends and colleagues with whom one can speak about everything, and which I too often have! They include John Roth, who has supported my work more than anyone over decades, and whom I first met because of our shared love for William James—a teacher of both of ours. And Dr. Robert Coles, who read my first book and said that we were "spiritual kin."

I remember Dr. Henry Krystal, a psychiatrist and founder of contemporary theory and treatment of trauma. Henry was also a survivor and treasured teacher about many important things. The book includes one moment.

In the same circle are Robert Ehrenreich, Alexandra Garbarini, Rachel Baum, Ken Waltzer, Kobi Kabalek, Anna Sheftel, Stacey Zembrzycki, Wendy Lower, Larry Langer, Malin Thor Tureby, Christine Schmidt, Ian Robinson, Tom Elliott, Ray Schnueringer, Jennifer Myers, Gigi Lincoln, and Steven High. And slightly younger friends/colleagues upon whose smarts and counsel I often relied: Charlotte Schallie, Lisa Peschel, Noah Shenker, Laen Avraham Dov Hershler, and more.

And there is forever Sid Bolkosky, my friend and brother and coconspirator in a hundred ways. And to whose memory this book is dedicated.

And, of course, the survivors some of whom are especially central in these pages as they were in my life: Agi Rubin, Abe Pasternak, Joe Oberlin, Abe Friedman, Mary Newman, Miriam Winter, Roma Solent, Henry Starkman, Irene Butter, and many, many more.

And generations of students who are far too many to name but from whom I learned as much as I taught. I think especially of my 2010 first-year seminar with whom I still occasionally meet. For reasons I won't say, we call our class the "space cadets." With love.

Young people. The source of so much hope and joy, even in these very dark times. Two were essential in my work on *REMNANTS* and especially in creating a viable performance video.

Jenna Sperling Reisenauer is my "bonus daughter" in the same way that Sid Bolkosky was my "bonus brother." And Myles Hoenes, a geyser of creativity and care.

And there are those I call the "theater peeps"—teachers, directors, fellow actors, fellow playwrights. They include David Ford, Mathew Paul Olmos, Stefanie Zadravec, Roland Tec, Suze Allen, Kate Mendeloff, Donny Riedel, and Ann Klautsch, with whom I directed the radio production of *REMNANTS* and who was more perfectionist than I was, which is impossible. Scott Weissman encouraged my first dramatic writing about survivors that led to three of the monologues in *REMNANTS*.

And the large and small organizations that made my work possible in so many ways: the Residential College of the University of Michigan where I taught and thrived; the United States Holocaust Memorial Museum; the Holocaust Educational Foundation of Northwestern University; Concordia University in Montreal and its Centre for Oral History and Digital Storytelling; the University of Michigan Society of Fellows; Fulbright Canada; Michigan Radio (WUOM-FM) and especially Harriet Teller, who oversaw the first formal production of *REMNANTS*; the Workshop on Interview Interpretation, which I initiated during the pandemic and now has members from the United States, Canada, Mexico, the United Kingdom, Holland, Sweden, Slovakia, Poland, Romania, and Israel—depending on what day it is; Digital Media Commons at the University of Michigan and especially Jacques Mersereau; The Marsh Theater of San Francisco; the Essay and Personal Memoir class, overseen by Eleanor Linn, at the University of Michigan Osher Lifelong Learning Institute, where most of the essays in *What Remains* were first read.

Some were also performed as dramatic monologues in David Ford's class at The Marsh.

And my gratitude to the whole team at Wayne State University Press as well as to the two outside reviewers, who wrote about this book as though they were my mother.

And, as always, Nancy, who is the ground of everything.

About the Author

Henry Hank Greenspan is an emeritus psychologist, oral historian, and playwright at the University of Michigan. He is the author of the seminal *On Listening to Holocaust Survivors: Beyond Testimony* as well as the play *REMNANTS*, which was originally distributed on National Public Radio in the United States and has since been performed on more than three hundred stages worldwide. He has been a Fulbright Research Chair, a recipient of the Distinguished Achievement Award in Holocaust Studies from the Holocaust Educational Foundation, and a recipient of two Michigan Public Broadcasting Focus Awards.

Photo Credit: Nancy Hart Greenspan